DO BUSINESS

MINISTRY IN THE **MARKETPLACE**

WHERE FAITH AND BUSINESS **CONVERGE**

DO BUSINESS

MINISTRY IN THE **MARKETPLACE**

WHERE FAITH AND BUSINESS **CONVERGE**

VINCENT ROBINSON

DO BUSINESS

Ministry in the MARKETPLACE

ISBN: 978-1-7360064-8-1
Published by Robinson Media and Publishing Mobile, AL
www.kingdom-wealth.org
www.vrministries.org
www.rightwayccc.org

Subjects: **Business I Empowerment I Entrepreneurship**

Printed in the United States of America

This Book's Goal

There is a goal that I am shooting for with this book. It's not to teach you strategies on business growth and expansion, although through the application of this book's content, that's going to happen—automatically. It's also not necessarily to motivate or explain to you how to capitalize on business opportunities. Although, again, if you simply do what's inside, that's going to happen all by itself.

My first goal is to get you to realize that the Word of God is given to us for victory in all areas of our lives. We do not have to sit our relationship with God aside in any dealings, especially those pertaining to business.

The second goal of this book is to get you to see that there is something special about a Believer doing business God's way that can catapult you above your peers in the marketplace. Most of what most businesspersons relentlessly grind and hustle for, God has already set up to automatically happen for the Kingdom businessperson, **"But seek first his Kingdom and His righteousness, and all these things will be given to you as well"** (Matt. 6:33 NIV). That key is not to work hard but to work smart: **Ye have not chosen me, but I have chosen you, and ordained you, that ye should go and bring forth fruit, and that your fruit should remain"** (John 15:16).

The final goal of this book is to get you to see work from God's perspective. Yes, God gave man work. Second Thessalonians 3:10-12 (NIV) says, "For even when we were with you, we gave you this rule: **'The one who is unwilling to work shall not eat.'** We hear that some among you are idle and disruptive. They are not busy; they are busybodies. Such people we command and urge in the Lord Jesus Christ to settle down and earn the food they eat." So work is a part of man's existence.

Even Adam had work to do in the garden, but not the way that we think: "And the Lord God took the man, and put him into the garden of Eden **to dress it and to keep it"** (Gen. 2:15). This scripture has the main goal that this book is shooting for, and that goal is for you to see work the way God originally gave it to man. You see, the marketplace is not just a place of work, and it's more than a nine-to-five—**it's a mission field that you are assigned to**. It is a place that is missing and needs the presence and order of God, and God needs ambassadors who understand and see the marketplace as a Kingdom assignment. Work is simply the name of the tool that God uses to get Believers in, and, ultimately, we are on assignment. What others call work, to Believers, is God sending us to dress and keep. And as a result of getting Him into the system, we receive rewards and benefits.

This is where my goals lie: in teaching you that work from God to man has always been regarded as dressing and keeping. If you can pivot and give new meaning to what you call work and see it from God's view, you go to work with a different goal in mind. You realize that it's all a setup to get God in.

TABLE OF CONTENTS

Preface

The Caution of Rebuilding Babel

I am convinced that the building of the Tower of Babel was not directly wrong. Stick with me: the motive for building it was what was wrong. The order from God from the beginning was to be fruitful, multiply, replenish, subdue, and have dominion. Notice the words *multiply* (make more of) and *replenish* (to perpetually renew and supply). What made building the tower wrong was that man was supposed to go out into all the earth and establish God's Kingdom. They were to expand heaven, not build a tower in an effort to reach heaven. Pride, selfishness, and disobedience had them going in the wrong direction and doing their own thing.

However, the Tower of Babel was built from a principle that God Himself put into the earth for man's use. That principle is the principle of unity, where the commanded blessing of God lies:

> And the Lord said, Behold, the people **is one**, and they have all **one language**; and this they begin to do: and now nothing will be restrained from them, which they have imagined to do—Genesis 11:6. Behold, how good and how pleasant it is for brethren to dwell together **in unity**! It is like the precious ointment upon the head, that ran down upon the beard, even Aaron's beard: that went down to the skirts of his garments; as the dew of Hermon, and as the dew that descended upon the mountains of Zion**: for**

> **there** the Lord **commanded** the blessing, even life **for evermore (Ps. 133:1-3)**.

Just to give New Testament context to this same principle, Matthew 18:19 says, **"If any two shall agree on earth as in touching anything that they shall ask, it shall be done of the Father."** "Done of the Father" means that a supernatural ability and commanded blessing will rest on it.

So those builders of the tower were doing the right thing in principle, but the wrong way in practice because God did not tell them to build up to Him; He told them to go out (multiply, replenish, subdue, have dominion) and advance His Kingdom agenda into all the earth. The same instruction is given to us in the New Testament: **"Go ye into all the world, and preach the Gospel to every creature (Mark 16:15).** So the tower was a **"to-self"** build and not an **"unto God"** build. Had they taken that same approach with oneness and gone forth with a Kingdom Wealth Do Business mindset, imagine what would have become of them and where God's Kingdom would be today.

Is the Church, like the Babel builders, taking a "to-self" evangelism approach today? Are we tower builders? In Acts, we can see a small glimpse of the disciples almost doing the same thing before being filled with the Holy Spirit. I believe that had the angel not checked them in their position with the Holy Spirit, they would have taken the same evangelistic approach as the people in Genesis 11:

> And while they looked steadfastly toward heaven [tower build] as He went up, behold, two men stood by them in white apparel; Which also said, Ye men of Galilee, why stand ye gazing up into heaven? this same Jesus, which is taken up from you into heaven, shall so come in like manner as ye have seen Him go into Heaven.

I see this as a corrective rebuke. Look at what they are doing. They are looking up, when the charge was to be a witness in Jerusalem, Judea, Samaria, and to the uttermost part of the world. Is this not a Babel situation? Had the builders of Babel been there when Jesus went up, I am sure they would have tried to build a tower there. Verse 12 then says, "Then returned they unto Jerusalem from the mount called Olivet, which is from Jerusalem a sabbath day's journey." This is where they were supposed to be in the first place. The charge was to tarry in Jerusalem until they were endued with power. They were a sabbath journey's away from where they were supposed to be. All of this had to be corrected before they received power, or else, I believe we would have seen Babel all over again.

But my question that we must consider is whether the Church is functioning in a form of disobedience that has her operating as a semblance of Babel. Sadly, many Christians are building towers of Babel and either don't know or don't care. The assignment of the Church and those in the Kingdom is **to advance**, by doing the business of the Kingdom on earth. **We should be economically evangelizing the world.** Christians do not understand the **economic assignment** given to the Church for Earth. And if there are only good conferences and mid-week and Sunday services but no action of operating economically, we could possibly be in a repeat of rebuilding Babel: **"And Jesus came and spake unto them, saying, All power is given unto Me in heaven and in earth. Go ye therefore" (Matt. 28:18-19a).** The power was given to "go ye," which is out. Not "go ye up," which is Babel. The word "therefore" also designates how they were supposed to go. This word placement pronounces that we first look back to what was there before moving forward. And if we look back, Jesus said all power was given unto Him, which means that the going was predicated on having power. So the power was given to the Church for going "out" not going "up." Up would be the result or by-product of going out: **"But ye shall receive power, after that the Holy Ghost is come upon you: and ye shall be witnesses unto Me both in Jerusalem, and in all Judaea, and in Samaria, and unto the uttermost part of the earth" (Acts 1:8).**

There is an institution side of the Church for teaching, training, and spiritual growth, but there is also an economic organizational side of the Church that happens once the people in the Church leave out to do what *should* be the business of the Kingdom throughout the week. These two are equally important, because they reinforce one another: **"And I say unto you, Make to yourselves friends of the mammon of unrighteousness; that, when ye fail, they may receive you into everlasting habitations" (Luke 16:9).** Now read that in the New Living Translation: **"Here's the lesson: Use your worldly resources to benefit others and make friends. Then, when your possessions are gone, they will welcome you to an eternal home."** But how can we use the resources when we as an institution teach to stay away from the world?

God uses the Body of Christ in the Church in different spaces and arenas—this is the Church as an organism. We are individually endowed with spiritual gifts, natural talents, and acquired skills to prosper and then use our lives to point to the one and true Savior. This is how we do the business of the Kingdom. Our hands should be touching and causing things to increase. We should leave in every space we enter an impression that testifies that the Lord has been in this place.

Introduction

The World

Do we really want to hear what the Lord prayed about us? And do we really want to know what God's agenda for the Church is? Lastly, are we really ready to do the work of the Kingdom? As Believers, we often hear about the distinction between the Church and "the world." We know that the world, in many ways, is at odds with the Kingdom of God. Yet, in His prayer before going to the cross, Jesus made it clear that His desire was not to remove the Church from the world but to send us into it. Jesus prayed, **"I pray not that thou shouldest take them out of the world, but that thou shouldest keep them from the evil" (John 17:11-15).** This profound truth reveals that while we are not of the world, we are very much in the world, and our mission is to influence it for the Kingdom.

As Believers, our mission is to have a preserving, illuminating influence in the world. Jesus did not call us to withdraw into religious bubbles, but to engage the world in such a way that our presence makes a difference: **"You are the salt of the earth."** But if the salt loses its saltiness, how can it be made salty again? It is no longer good for anything, except to be thrown out and trampled underfoot. **"You are the light of the world."** A town built on a hill cannot be hidden. Neither do people light a lamp and put it under a bowl. Instead, they put it on its stand, and it gives light to everyone in the house. In the same way, **"Let your light shine before others,** that they may see your good deed and glorify your Father in Heaven"

(Matt. 5:13-16 NIV). I don't understand the position the Church takes as it pertains to the world. We stand outside the world and condemn what God has given to us as an assignment. He has literally made us the preservative and light that the world needs and then put the Church in a position **in the world** where it could be seen. He didn't hide us—He placed us high. He made the Church to be an example to be followed. The Church was sent and should come with answers and solutions. **"For God so loved the world that He gave His one and only Son, that whoever believes in Him shall not perish but have eternal life. [17] For God did not send His Son into the world to condemn the world, but to save the world through Him" (John 3:16-17 NIV)**. These verses are a clear call for the Church to be engaged with the world, bringing the influence of God's Kingdom into every corner of society. **Salt** that loses its saltiness is useless, and light hidden under a basket fails its purpose. In the same way, when the Church withdraws from the world, whether out of fear, comfort, or a misguided belief that it should remain isolated, there are profound consequences.

When the Church retreats from the world, it abandons its role as a transformational force in society. In business, politics, education, entertainment, and social systems, the absence of Kingdom values leaves a vacuum that gets filled with corruption, greed, and brokenness. Instead of being a force for good, the Church, by disengaging, allows other forces to shape the world. This is the danger of no salt—the very essence of our influence and purpose.

Jesus calls us to be the **light** of the world, illuminating the darkness with the truth, love, and justice of the Kingdom. When the Church fails to engage the world, it fails to shine this light in areas of darkness, whether those are injustices, poverty, broken systems, or personal suffering. The world needs the light of Christ, but if the Church remains hidden, choosing safety and isolation over engagement, that light is concealed, and people remain in darkness. When the Church stays within its own walls and avoids the spaces where the most brokenness exists, whether in the workplace, government, media, or other areas, it denies people the chance to encounter the transforming power of Christ. We are called to step into difficult and dark places, bringing hope, truth, and the message of reconciliation. Matthew 5:14 makes it clear: "a city set on a hill cannot be hidden," and neither can the Church.

The Church desires and prays to see change, but hasn't realized that it is the carrier of it.

Imagine a world devoid of the Church's influence. When Christian leaders, entrepreneurs, and professionals fail to engage in the marketplace, ethical standards decline, integrity is compromised, and the moral fabric of communities weakens. The Church, by neglecting its role as salt and light, leaves society vulnerable to values that undermine human dignity, justice, and righteousness. But Jesus specifically sent His disciples into the world to be agents of transformation. The Church is not called to merely exist within the four walls of a building; it is called to impact communities, industries, governments, and every aspect of culture.

Throughout His ministry, Jesus actively engaged with the world around Him. He didn't isolate Himself from sinners, tax collectors, and those considered unclean by religious standards. Instead, He sat at their tables, went into their homes, and met them where they were. This was not to condone sin, but to bring the redemptive message of the Kingdom into every sphere of life. Jesus didn't avoid the world's brokenness; He sought it out to bring healing: "When Jesus heard that, he said unto them, **'They that be whole need not a physician, but they that are sick. . . . For I am not come to call the righteous, but sinners to repentance'" (Matt. 9:12-13).** In the same way, we are called to enter into the world's broken systems, whether in business, education, politics, or culture, and bring the hope of the Gospel with us.

Just as Jesus was sent by the Father into the world to fulfill His purpose, so, too, are we sent by Christ. The Great Commission in Matthew 28:18-20 (NIV) commands us to **"go and make disciples of all nations."** The word "go" is critical. It implies action, movement, and engagement with the world outside the Church.

It's quite ironic that we are staying away from the thing that Jesus said He spent His time teaching on so that we might be in it and be effective, without being affected. Our mission is not limited to preaching the Gospel on Sundays or at Church events. It is a daily calling to live out our faith **in every sphere of influence**. Whether it's in the marketplace, neighborhoods, or social circles, we are on assignment. The Church is God's chosen vehicle to carry His message of redemption to a lost and dying world. Every Believer is called to live on mission, participating in the advancement of God's Kingdom on earth.

We have orders! And those orders are for being in the world. Jesus made it clear that while we are sent into the world, we are not to be conformed to its patterns. In John 17:14-16 (NIV), He prayed, **"I have given them your word, and the world has hated them, for they are not of the world any more than I am of the world. My prayer is not that you take them out of the world but that you protect them from the evil one."** This distinction is crucial. We are in the world, but our values, identity, and citizenship belong to another Kingdom. As we engage the world, we are called to maintain a Kingdom mindset. Our influence comes from our difference, not from blending in. The more we reflect Christ in our actions, character, and values, the more the world will see the hope of the Gospel through us.

When the Church understands its mandate to go into the world, it becomes a transformative force. Acts 17:6 (NIV) records that early Christians were accused of "turning the world upside down." Their influence was so profound that it challenged societal norms, religious traditions, and even political structures. For too long, many Christians have viewed business as a "secular" domain, separate from the spiritual call of the Church. However, the marketplace is one of the most influential arenas in shaping culture, ethics, and how communities operate. By not entering this space with purpose and boldness, Christians allow systems driven by profit over people, unethical practices, and unjust power dynamics to dominate.

Today, the Church is called to have that same world-changing influence. Whether it's advocating for justice, showing compassion to the marginalized, or demonstrating excellence in business and leadership, the Church's role is to bring the values of the Kingdom into every sector of society. We are called to influence culture, not to be controlled by it. Our faith should impact how we work, how we lead, and how we interact with the world around us. Jesus didn't send us into the world to fend for ourselves. He empowered us with the Holy Spirit to be His witnesses. Acts 1:8 (NIV) says, **"But you will receive power when the Holy Spirit comes on you; and you will be My witnesses in Jerusalem, and in all Judea and Samaria, and to the ends of the earth."** The Holy Spirit equips us with the boldness, wisdom, and discernment we need to navigate the complexities of the world. We are not sent into the world powerless. We carry the same Spirit that raised Christ from the dead. This gives us the authority and strength to not only survive in the world but to thrive as agents of change. The Holy Spirit empowers us to break strongholds, influence hearts, and bring the light of Christ into dark places.

Ultimately, the Church's mission in the world is to bring Heaven to earth. In Luke 11:2 it says, "Thy Kingdom come. Thy will be done, **as in Heaven, so in earth**." Our goal is to establish God's will on earth in every sphere of life. As we go into the world, we are called to model what Heaven looks like—where love, justice, peace, and righteousness reign. We bring Heaven to earth when we operate in integrity in business, when we stand for truth in our communities, and when we extend compassion to those in need. Every time we align our actions with God's heart, we advance His Kingdom in the world. This is the high calling of the Church, and it requires us to be fully engaged in the world around us.

Jesus didn't pray for the Church to be taken out of the world. Instead, He prayed for us to be protected and empowered as we go into the world to fulfill our mission. The world needs the Church more than ever, and the Church's mission is far from complete. We are called to be salt and light, to bring hope and transformation to every corner of society. As we embrace this calling, we fulfill the heart of Christ, who came not to condemn the world but to save it. Let us go boldly into the world, knowing that we are sent by the One who has already overcome it.

Today, more than ever, the Church needs to embrace its role as a force for good in the world. This requires courage, intentionality, and a willingness to engage with areas that may be challenging, broken, or even uncomfortable. Whether it's in business, politics, education, or social justice, the Church must lead by example, embodying the principles of love, truth, integrity, and justice. God has uniquely gifted His people to be agents of transformation, not just in the spiritual realm, but in every aspect of life. The world needs Christian leaders, businesspeople, educators, and professionals who are committed to using their influence to bring about change. By stepping into the marketplace and other spaces of influence, we fulfill our call to be salt and light, preserving what is good, exposing what is broken, and offering solutions that reflect the wisdom and grace of God.

Chapter 1
Marketplace Ministry

Simon Peter answered, "You are the Messiah, the Son of the living God." Jesus replied, "You are blessed, Simon son of John, because my Father in Heaven has revealed this to you. You did not learn this from any human being. Now I say to you that you are Peter (which means 'rock'), and upon this rock I will build My Church, and all the powers of hell will not conquer it. And I will give you the keys of the Kingdom of Heaven. Whatever you forbid on earth will be forbidden in heaven, and whatever you permit on earth will be permitted in heaven."

—Matthew 16:16-19 NLT

The Church has been and is being slighted. I am not speaking in terms of the building—we have progressed in having excellent and amazing facilities. When I say Church, I am speaking about the people, the ecclesia, the called-out ones that collectively make up and become the Church. Many of these people have yet to have been taught in fullness what the Church is and how the Church has been called to function in the earth as a Kingdom until Christ returns . . . **"as in Heaven so in earth" (Luke 11:3)**.

What are the Church's orders? What was and is still God's agenda for creating man and placing him on Earth? Does God have or want anything to do with the systems and things that run the world? And if so, how does the Church fit within the scope of those things? Are we just waiting for a day when God's Bride will be saved unto eternity, or have God's people been assigned to a daily activity of doing and being a mission-mobile Church, the type of Church that doesn't consist of a choir, ushers, altar calls, soup kitchens, food drives, etc., but a Church that goes into systems and changes orders, and takes dominion . . . **"These that have turned the world upside down are come hither also" (Acts 17:6b)**.

The Church has been slighted by the understanding that it has been equipped, anointed, and commissioned to go into the economy. When we say the Kingdom of God, we are dealing with more than just God's way of doing things in our personal lives. This statement far exceeds that. This statement means that we are dealing with the Church in operation. I like to call it Kingdom Economics. But this statement has been disparaged into only meaning "a righteous way of living." What we are talking about is a Kingdom—a king and his governing domain. The Kingdom of God is a statement of operation and government. It extends far beyond just you personally. The Kingdom of God consists of power and demonstration. It's not a New Testament phenomenon. We see the Kingdom of God in Genesis in the orders that were given to the first man: **"And God blessed them, and God said unto them, Be fruitful, and multiply, and replenish the earth, and subdue it: and <u>have dominion</u> over the fish of the sea, and over the fowl of the air, and over every living thing that moveth upon the earth" (Gen. 1:28)**.

> Marketplace Believers maintain their integrity in competitive environments.

The Church has been commissioned as the answer to the world's problems. The problems of this world, the government, and the marketplace cannot be solved on the same level as their existence. They need a higher level of wisdom that comes from a higher governing domain. These places need Godly resolve and Godly wisdom, and God has given that to the Church as its ministry—**marketplace ministry**. This phrase, *marketplace ministry*, is a foreign and blasphemous word to use or teach in the Church, yet from Monday through Saturday and even on Sundays, most of the Church is operating inside of the world's economy. The Church cannot continue to hide behind the phrase, "The world hates us," when, in truth, our actions do not align with who we claim to be. That is what people hate about the Church: hypocrisy. When I look at the Bible, it was the religious and the demonic who didn't want to see Jesus coming. But he drew crowds of unsaved and altered systems as He evangelized the world.

Now, this is not just about work or doing a good job. The Church has something to offer that gives us a compelling edge. Remember Daniel, who I mentioned earlier? The Bible says his excellent spirit was the reason he got promoted over 123 others (Dan. 6:1-3). And when they could find no occasion against him, they sought to bring accusation against Daniel in his governing affairs, and they could find none there either (vs. 4). The scripture says that he was faithful, and there was no error of fault found in him.

Daniel reveals to us some principles of marketplace ministry:

- Integrity and ethical behavior: Daniel was not just good at what he did; it was the twin of who he was. Daniel had great character and integrity and was accountable for his actions. And when he was challenged, no fault was found. Colossians 3:23 encourages us to work heartily as for the Lord and not for men. Applying this, we can ensure honesty, fairness, and integrity in all our business dealings. The Believer has to see the importance and value of protecting their integrity. I gained an understanding of this when I was in business and early in ministry. No matter what, I remained true to integrity, and just like the scripture said, it protected and guided me every time. When you have integrity, it guides your behaviors. Integrity and behavior are akin to each other.

- Servant leadership: Jesus taught us to lead by serving others. He sat down, called the twelve disciples over to him, and said, **"Whoever wants to be first must take last place and be the servant of everyone else" (Mark 9:35 NLT).** In a business environment, this might mean prioritizing the needs and growth of your team members. This behavior is absent in the marketplace and provides the Believer an amazing opportunity to shine the light of Christ. It is ordinarily assumed that the person will miss their moment in doing such. But not in the Kingdom. In the Kingdom, when we work for the service and advancing of others, we are really employing God to go to work on our behalf. **"Serve wholeheartedly, as if you were serving the Lord, not people, because you know that the Lord will reward each one for whatever good they do, whether they are slave or free" (Eph. 6:7-8 NIV).**

- Excellence and stewardship: Whatever we do, we should do it with excellence, as a reflection of our commitment to God (Matt. 25:14-30).
- Community building: Caring for and nurturing relationships within our professional circles reflects God's love and fosters a supportive and thriving community. **"Be kindly affectioned one to another with brotherly love; in honour preferring one another; not slothful in business; fervent in spirit; serving the Lord" (Rom. 12:10-11).**

You will face many challenges when your aim is to be a demonstration of Christ in the marketplace, but you can overcome them. Balancing faith and business isn't always easy. Questions of compromise and ethics frequently arise. However, drawing strength from prayer, seeking wise counsel, and staying rooted in scripture can provide much-needed guidance. **"This should be your ambition: to live a quiet life, minding your own business and doing your own work, just as we told you before. As a result, people who are not Christians will trust and respect you, and you will not need to depend on others for enough money to pay your bills" (I Thess. 4:11-12 TLB).**

In business, you'll often face ethical dilemmas where compromising your values might seem like the easier path to success. It is in these moments that you seek God's guidance through prayer and immerse yourself in Scripture to find strength and direction. Believers often overlook the advantage that they have with the Holy Spirit. He often becomes the last resort rather than the first. His purpose in the life of the Believer is to strengthen, comfort, teach, lead, guide, show you things to come, and bring all things the Believer has learned back to their remembrance. Just look at the immense advantage the Believer has with the Holy Spirit! But often in business, the Believer still sits idly by on the sideline, anxiously waiting to play his or her part in life. Further, competitiveness can sometimes push businesses toward unethical practices to stay ahead. But we don't have to break rank to get ahead.

Marketplace Believers maintain their integrity in competitive environments. God has already granted you good success (Josh. 1:8), and a good life (Eph. 2:10). Your security is in doing right. Short-term gains from unethical practices can damage long-term reputation and success. Commit to excellence in your products/services, which naturally sets you apart in a competitive market. There should be a quality that comes from the stewarding and maintenance of the Believer that stands paramount. Trust in God's Provision. Maintain faith that God will honor your commitment to integrity (Prov. 22:1).

Another challenge is the peer pressure or cultural norms that conflict with your faith-based values. You cannot wilt in the face of adversity. Stand firm in your convictions. Be clear about your values and do not waver under pressure. **"So, my dear brothers and sisters, be strong and immovable. Always work enthusiastically for the Lord, for you know that nothing you do for the Lord is ever useless" (I Cor. 15:58 NLT).** Use these challenges as an opportunity to share your perspective and influence the culture positively. Another way to circumvent challenges is to surround yourself with mentors and colleagues who share your values and can offer support and accountability. Surround yourself with like-minded individuals and partners who understand and respect your values. Marketplace ministry is not a stand-alone adventure. Even Jesus sent the disciples out two by two.

Faith in the Marketplace

While Paul was waiting for them in Athens, he was greatly distressed to see that the city was full of idols. So he reasoned in the synagogue with both Jews and God-fearing Greeks, as well as **in the marketplace** day by day with those who happened to be there.

—**Acts 17:16-17**

Believers are not only called to participate in culture but are accountable for leading and shaping it. Very few Believers who have businesses have those grounded on Kingdom principles. By *grounded,* I mean that the Word of God and their relationship with God cross over into how they do business. This is because they put separation between their personal relationship with God and business. They may also have not been taught that biblical principles are given to achieve success in the marketplace. Another problem is that they see business as personal and not purposeful. Our purpose in life comes from God, and He gave us purpose for life and Kingdom fulfillment, **"For I say, through the grace given unto me, to every man that is among you, not to think of himself more highly than he ought to think; but to think soberly, according as God hath dealt to every man the measure of faith" (Rom. 12:3).** Purpose is a package deal. It includes what you desire and what God wants. We can't make business personal, because by doing so we neglect the very purpose for God's giving. Matthew 5:16b says, "That they may see your good works, and glorify your Father which is in heaven." Faith isn't given just as a way of living; the faith of a Kingdom-preneur should be seen. And when it is seen, God gets the glory. When we make business personal and don't engage the principals of the Word in business, we not only cheat the business of supernatural engagement, but we also cheat God out of His intended desire. How can we accept God sharing His blessing but not bring God alongside the functioning of our business models?

It is not difficult to recognize other faiths in the marketplace. Most of them have certain clothing that identifies them. For the Believer, our faith may not be as recognizable as others' when it comes to our outer garments. The distinguishing difference for the Kingdom-preneur should be seen in the operation of our faith lived out, and should without question leave no resolve as to who we represent. Take Joseph for instance—even though Jospeh dressed like he was a citizen of Egypt, there was no question that his faith was in the Almighty God, **"And Pharaoh said unto Joseph, Forasmuch as God hath shewed thee all this, there is none so discreet and wise as thou art: thou shalt be over my house, and according unto thy word shall all my people be ruled: only in the throne will I be greater than thou. And Pharaoh said unto Joseph, See, I have set thee over all the land of Egypt. And Pharaoh took off his ring from his hand, and put it upon Joseph's hand, and arrayed him in vestures of fine linen, and put a gold chain about his neck" (Gen. 31:39-42).** The point I am inserting is that our faith should be evident in all that we do. The Word isn't just what we study, it's how we live. Romans 1:17 says, **"For therein is the righteousness of God revealed from faith to faith: as it is written, <u>The just shall live by faith</u>."** If it is not evident that the hand of God is on your business dealing, something is off. Remember the scripture said that they should see your good works. We are often trying to get people to hear about a God they do not know. **They don't hear until they see: "Then said Jesus unto him, Except ye see signs and wonders, ye will not believe" (John 4:48).** But if they can see His hand at work on the life of a Kingdom-preneur, they now have undeniable proof of His ability. And here is where faith and business converge: when a Believer is in purpose and operating in business through faith, it lays the foundation for lives to be impacted so transformation can take place.

Faith is not just a way of Believing God. Faith is a way of living, doing, and being morally accountable. **"For we walk by faith [we regulate our lives and conduct ourselves by our conviction or belief respecting man's relationship to God and divine things, with trust and holy fervor; thus we walk] not by sight or appearance" (II Cor. 5:7 AMPC).** You have a social responsibility to uphold in the marketplace as a representative of the Kingdom. An in-corporate social responsibility and ethical practices are core components of your business model. You should uphold the following:

1. **Building trust and credibility:** This is what gives you the advantage and what is called the "marketplace edge." Businesses that operate with integrity and honesty build a strong reputation and trust with customers, employees, and partners and have the greatest impact. Trust leads to customer loyalty, better employee retention, and strong partnerships.

2. **Creating a positive work culture:** Who doesn't want to be served? We often assume that biblical principles will be rejected. However, applying biblical principles removes partiality, creates balance, employs servant leadership, and builds a community that fosters a positive work environment.

3. **Encouraging long-term success:** The Bible says that God has given unto us all things that pertain to life and godliness (II Pet. 1:3). So the Bible isn't just a book written to us about how to have a relationship with God. It's also a book that teaches and guides us in how to conduct our affairs in life and business. What the Marketplace Believer must realize is that ethical and sustainable practices lead to long-term success rather than short-lived gains from unethical means. And the impact ensures the longevity of your business and its steady growth over time.

4. **Fulfilling a greater purpose:** Running a business on Kingdom principles gives a deeper sense of purpose and fulfillment beyond just profit. The Word can't return void. It prospers in the thing for which it was sent. Here again, we are blinded from the impact that the Word has the ability to perform in the Marketplace. Its spiritual dimension can open doors and create opportunities beyond human efforts.

5. **Reaping divine favor and blessing:** The Marketplace Believer should expect to multiply (Deut. 28:1-12). Faithful adherence to biblical principles invites God's blessings and favor upon your business.

Remember that every challenge you face is an opportunity to stand firm in your faith and show the world the power and wisdom of living by God's Word. Your consistency in faith and business can be a powerful testimony and inspire others to follow a similar path.

The Institution vs. the Organism

There is a movement that is missing from the Church that directly correlates to the advancing and assignment of the Kingdom. The Church has two arms. It has an institutional arm and an organism arm. The organism arm of the Church is the movement that the Church heavily lacks, and it directly correlates to the complete fulfillment of the assignment of the Church of going and preaching the **Gospel of the <u>Kingdom of God</u>**: **"Now after that John was put in prison, Jesus came into Galilee, preaching the Gospel of the Kingdom of God, and saying, The time is fulfilled, and <u>the Kingdom of God is at hand</u>: repent ye, and believe the Gospel" (Mark 1:14-15).** In this statement lies both arms of the Church. Ironically, the focus has only been put on the institution and the preaching of the Gospel but not the commission of establishing the Kingdom of God (on earth as it is in Heaven), which belongs to the organism arm of the Church. With only one arm in operation, the Church is handicapped and in operation as an amputee, when she has been empowered and commissioned to function as a whole body: **"For as we have many members in one body, and all members have not the same office so we, being many, are one body in Christ, and every one members one of another (Rom. 12:4-5).**

Most understand the Church as an Institution. *Institution* generally refers to a structured, established organization or foundation that operates under a set of rules, guidelines, and traditions. To the Church, the institution involves a permanent structure where Christians gather weekly and bi-weekly to be taught the Word and trained in the things of God. As the institution, the people come, serve, build community, and receive from God. But as the organism, those same people that received from God are now educated, empowered, and equipped with the Kingdom **to go out** as the Church into the world to carry out the ministry to which they were administered. So in contrast, considering these entities as an "organism" focuses on their dynamic, living, and adaptive qualities. Understanding and balancing both approaches can be crucial.

Church as an Organism is the ministry of the Gospel of the Kingdom to the world through the Believer in the marketplace, with the operation of spiritual gifts, the working of natural talents, and the practice of acquired skills, for running kingdoms, reconciling people, subverting systems, and reclaiming things for the glory of God: **"And all of this is a gift from God, who brought us back to himself through Christ. And God has given us this task of reconciling people to Him. For God was in Christ, reconciling the world to himself, no longer counting people's sins against them. And he gave us this wonderful message of reconciliation. So we are Christ's ambassadors; God is making his appeal through us. We speak for Christ when we plead, "Come back to God" (II Cor. 5:18-20 NLT)!**

It could also be considered the missions arm of the Church, the arm of the Church that is found outside of the four walls. There is a difference between the arm of institution and the arm of organism. They are interdependent on each other, but their characteristics are different. While institutions provide stability and order, the organism perspective brings adaptability, expansion, and progression. When the two are at work, the Church becomes a resilient and innovative organization.

Institution to Organism

The **institution** is where you learn of your dominion.

The **organism** is you taking dominion.

The **institution** is where you learn the principles.

The **organism** is where you work the principles.

The **institution** is where you learn of Jesus.

The **organism** is where you share Jesus.

The **institution** is where you gain power.

The **organism** is where you demonstrate power.

The **institution** is where you sow seed.

The **organism** is where you reap the harvest.

The **institution** is for the saved soul.

The **organism** is for reaching souls.

The **institution** gathers in a building.

The **organism** is the building going into the field.

The **institution** comes away from the world.

The **organism** goes into the world.

The **institution** is where you practice the play.

The **organism** is where you play the game.

The **institution** plants the seed.

The **organism** produces the harvest.

The **institution** is to the personal growth of the person

The **organism** is for the introduction of a people to a Person.

Organism to Institution

The **organism** reaches the harvest (goes out).

Then the **institution** cares for the harvest (as they come in).

The **organism** is the laborer of the harvest.

The **institution** is the steward to the harvest.

The **organism** fishes.

Then the **institution** cleans.

The **organism** is anointed to reach.

Then the **institution** is anointed raise.

It is important that these two work together and don't cross over into each other's lane, and here's why: The administration of the two are totally different. **"And there are differences of administrations, but the same Lord. 6 And there are diversities**

of operations, but it is the same God which worketh all in all" (I Cor. 12:5-6). One is the direct demonstration of Christ, while the other is for teaching and growing the Believer in Christ. When you demonstrate, you are an example, so when you are seen, they ask, "Why?": **"Let your light so shine before men that they may see your moral excellence your praiseworthy, noble, good deeds and recognize honor praise glorify your Father Who is in Heaven" (Matt. 5:16 AMPC).** Sadly, many Christians have the Word in their mouth but absent in their actions. The organism doesn't have to talk, because the performance speaks for itself. From the organism, they should want to ask, "Why?"... "How?"... and "Explain?" The Hebrews boys were a prime example of the Church in operation; my definition of what the organism is. It's the Word of God in operation in the marketplace.

Believers should be the first people considered for the raise, running the Fortune 500 companies, leading and championing in the marketplace, and being awarded for remarkable numbers and gains. Unfortunately, we don't see that as missions for Christ, because the Church is blind to this organism call. So, we, like everyone else, go to work, clock in, work hours, and clock out. It's not about a Kingdom assignment; it's about a check, not understanding that with the Kingdom assignment comes promotion and advancement. We made the absolute of witnessing as knocking on doors, when the average Believer is out in the world five to seven hours a day, five days a week on average. We are waiting to knock on doors on Saturday while passing by the door that Jesus knocks on, the heart of man (Rev. 3:20), hundreds of times daily and possibly thousands of times weekly. The organism is in the mission field daily, so imagine what is missed Monday through Friday when we only have a Saturday door-knocking mentality. That's why the Believer must view their work/career as a mission field. Work is God's systematic way of inserting Himself into the world's system through the Believer as the organism of His Church. And simultaneously, as you do your work, God causes you to be blessed and elevated. It's His way of getting seed and harvest—increase to you, glory and souls for Him.

The institution and the organism are equally important and needed of each other: **"But now hath God set the members every one of them in the body, as it hath pleased him. And if they were all one member, where were the body? But now are they many members, yet but one body (I Cor. 12:18-20).** Unfortunately, this revelation of the Church being an institution to live people and being in operation as an organism for Kingdom expansion, an organism assigned to the world to restore things back to the Father, has gotten lost. The Church rests and focuses heavily on institutions, as it should. However, we should not be coming up short on the actions. It is as the organism that God's power is really demonstrated: **"And they went forth, and preached every where, the Lord working with them, and confirming the word with signs following. Amen (Mark 16:20) . . . and where gifts get their greatest operation, A man's gift maketh room for him, and bringeth him before great men" (Prov. 18:16).** For example, Jesus met this woman at the well and prophesied over her life. She became fully convinced, so much so, that she went and brought the entire city to Jesus. Jesus didn't have to outreach to that city. The city was in the woman at the well. But had He waited to see if she was going to arrive at the institution, He could have possibly missed the moment. This is because **the Institution is for gathering—the Organism is for going.**

When Church is taught as an organism, you often hear circulating that the teaching is heresy, misguided, off, and new age. That is because the administration of the organism arm is different than that of the institution. This is also why you find these two arms at odds with each other. Many Believers that are called to the organism struggle to be free in it because it seems contradictory to what they receive on Sunday in its operation. There are others who feel out of touch with the institution because they are called to the organism, and vice versa. When I was called to ministry, I heard the Lord say that I was an in-house Levite. That sounds very churchy, but I knew exactly what God was saying. Everything that I do deals with the institution. I have pastors who have side businesses apart from the Church, but God was telling me that my life would not be structured the same way. Everything I do is in the institution and from the institution. I do teach the organism, but it is still from the institution. I think that this is very important for the Believer to know because they could have all the right tools, but they are being used in the wrong place. Joseph and Daniel were both prophets, but their gifts were appointed to the political arena. You fit somewhere, but where is the discovery.

Blind Salvation

Satan, who is the god of this world, has blinded the minds of those who don't believe. They are unable to see the glorious light of the Good News. They don't understand this message about the glory of Christ, who is the exact likeness of God.
—II Corinthians 4:4 NLT

> The Believer has tremendous impact on the marketplace through *power, position*, and *personage*.

When I say *blind salvation*, I am saying that the Church is short-sighted in understanding the fullness of salvation. Blind salvation is a salvation that points to only getting to Heaven, while ignoring the Kingdom responsibilities of the Believer that are assigned on Earth. Blind salvation is when Christians turn their backs on God's creation command of being fruitful, multiplying, and having dominion over all the earth. **The Kingdom of God is about going to Heaven.** The Kingdom of God is about establishing Heaven on Earth, through the replication of God's will, and the re-establishing of God's system over the earth.

Salvation birthed you not only into a new life, but into a new system of operation: **"Jesus answered and said unto him, Verily, verily, I say unto thee Except a man be born again, he cannot see the Kingdom of God (John 3:3). Go, stand and speak in the temple to the people all the words of <u>this life"</u> (Acts 5:20)**. Because there is no full revelation of salvation, the enemy can manipulate people into opposition against the system of God. **"Every kingdom divided against itself is brought to desolation; and a house divided against a house falleth" (Luke 11:17b)**. Because of this blindness, the kingdom of darkness prevails rather than the Kingdom of light. Believers need eyes of understanding (Eph. 1:16-19).

So what is the purpose of salvation? The primary purpose of salvation was to restore **power**, **position**, and **personhood**. Heaven is a byproduct of salvation, not the goal. Adam lost what he needed to govern Earth's affairs, and Jesus came to restore those things to man, so that in Christ we could carry out the mandate of the Kingdom—to occupy (do business, buy, sell, trade, carry out the Kingdom's agenda in the earth), which was to be fruitful, multiply, and replenish, until Christ returns. **Inside of the new man in Christ is a deposit of God's system of operation for His economy**, and this system has the capacity to subvert and dominate the world's system. **"Neither shall they say, Lo here! or, lo there! for, behold, the Kingdom of God is within you" (Luke 17:21).** Salvation has put man back to where he fell from, so he can pick up where Adam fell off. **"For if because of one man's trespass (lapse, offense) death reigned through that one, much more surely will those who receive [God's] overflowing grace (unmerited favor) and the free gift of righteousness [putting them into right standing with Himself] reign as kings in life through the one Man Jesus Christ (the Messiah, the Anointed One)" (Rom. 5:17 AMPC)**. God has not changed His mind or His agenda for why He created man and planted him on earth: **"Thy Kingdom come. Thy will be done, as in Heaven so in earth" (Luke 11:2).**

We made salvation the end-all. Name written in the Book of Life, place secured in Heaven. But salvation is just the door. No one gets to the restaurant and doesn't walk. The Church has been walking in salvation, the righteous teaching that comes from the institution. But now it is time for the Church to walk out salvation, and that is as the organism, into the world as Kingdom agents.

Now that you are born again, you should be able to see (perceive and understand) the Kingdom of God. I want to pause here and talk to the Christian who has been hearing and sensing that there was more to this, but because of the lack of teaching on this, you felt like you were sinning or falling away from God because you were keener on the business (the organism) than you were the institution. I want you to know that nothing is or was ever wrong with you. That is where your call, anointing, and spiritual IQ were intended to shine, and the reason I wrote this book. Too many Believers are distancing and leaving the Church from feeling dried out because they don't see themselves in the institution. And it's because they were created to function as the organism. And I know firsthand that because this knowledge is lacking in the Church, it is often un-spiritualized and even demonized. It's the Blind Salvation we are speaking of right now. This conglomerate of Believers isn't embraced by the Church like those who work in the institution. I want you to know that you are right where God needs you to be, and your spiritual cognizance has always been doing exactly what it was supposed to do. Prayerfully, now you will step fully into it, and be to the Church the exact arm you were supposed to be, and we so desperately need.

As we said earlier, the Kingdom is a system of operation that involves the restoration of people, places, and things back to their rightful owners. In order to make this happen, man needed power, position, and personhood. I did not want to turn this book into a Bible study; however, this is so important to the organism arm of the Church. I struggled with whether or not this fit this book, but I realized that Jesus did not send the disciples out into the world without these three concepts, so it would be unjust to the reader not to give you a well-rounded understanding of these.

> We are not just working for earthly success but for the advancement of God's Kingdom.

Let's look at **power**. Jesus came to restore power back to man. You need the power of God working in you as you go into the secular market. It was never the purpose of God that man work by his own will, strength, or might. **"Not by might, nor by power, but by My Spirit, saith the Lord of Hosts" (Zech. 4:6c).** Jesus was clear that it was the Father that was doing the work through Him (John 5:17). We are strong in the Lord and in the power of His might (Eph. 6:10), and not our own. This is where the assured success comes from **"of the exceeding greatness of His power to us-ward who believe,**

the working of His might power" (Eph. 1:19). You do not go without power. One of the biggest failures as Kingdom entrepreneurs is that we go into the workforce and lay aside who we are in Christ, not realizing that that is the thing that causes us to excel above our peers and the very reason why we go—to bring glory to God.

Power is necessary! It was commanded of the Apostles that they tarry until they received power, because it was the power that would enable them to provide witness (tangible, undeniable proof). Jesus did not want them to go without having the ability to produce. God needs us to produce, so He empowered us with the ability to do so. His name is on the line.

Power over the enemy: you have authority over the enemy **(Matt. 10:1, Luke 10:1 9, Col. 1:14, Heb. 1:14)**. **Power** as a son of God: this deals with having heaven's backing and exercising divine authority **(Matt. 16:19, John 1:12)**. **Power** in the might of Christ: you have authority in the Name that is above every name. The Name that has authority in heaven, in earth, and under the earth. The Name that demons obey. And the Name by which all things were made by and for **(John 16:23, Phil. 2:9-11, Eph. 6:10, Col. 1:16)**. **Power** over sin: this keeps you out of the wheelhouse of your flesh and allows you to lead proficiently **(Rom. 6:6-23, Col. 2:15)**. **Power** of the Holy Spirit: this empowers you in your gift(s) and anoints you to stand out and perform at a superior level **(Acts 1:8)**. **Power** to prosper and perform: Believers should stand out from the crowd, set the standard, and raise the bar **(Deut. 8:16, 28:13, Matt. 5:16, Mark 16:20, Tit. 2:7)**.

The world needs answers. The resolve to earth's affairs cannot be solved on the same level as their existence. Those answers have to come from the ones who have been empowered with a higher level of wisdom and knowledge. And that's you! God created you to solve problems: **"Now when they saw the boldness of Peter and John, and perceived that they were unlearned and ignorant men, they marvelled; and they took knowledge of them, that they had been with Jesus" (Acts 4:13).**

The next thing that salvation restored to us was our rightful **position**. The position is important because it has to do with reigning: **"For if because of one man's trespass (lapse, offense) death reigned through that one, much more surely will those who receive [God's] overflowing grace (unmerited favor) and the free gift of righteousness <u>[putting them into right standing with Himself] reign as kings in life</u> through the one Man Jesus Christ (the Messiah, the Anointed One)" (Rom. 5:17 AMPC).**

This book is different because we are not covering how you should live as a Christian. We are revealing that salvation is not limited to the spiritual realm, but extends to all spheres of life, including the marketplace. It is important that you recognize that your spiritual authority and dominion as a Believer also enables you to influence and lead effectively in the marketplace. It gives us confidence to operate from a position of strength and not fear. Knowing our position in Christ means we carry His authority into the marketplace, and this translates to making decisions boldly, initiating positive change, and leading with integrity. When we are grounded in our identity as saints, we are less likely to be swayed by ethical compromises or peer pressure. We can stand firm in our principles. We enter meetings or negotiations with the assurance that we have divine wisdom and favor. We lead our teams with the confidence that comes from knowing we are equipped and empowered by God.

POSITION EXAMPLE

Truett Cathy, the founder of Chick-fil-A, implemented business practices that were heavily influenced by his Christian faith. He kept the restaurant closed on Sundays, allowing employees to rest and worship. His leadership focused on integrity, service, and quality, aligning with the understanding of reigning with Christ's authority and grace. This not only led to the restaurant's success but also set a precedent for ethical business leadership.

The Believer's position is that we are made righteous: **"So by the obedience of one shall many be made righteous" (Rom. 5:19).** Therefore, we are guided by righteousness. Our righteousness in Christ should be reflected in our business practices. This means being honest, ethical, and fair in all dealings. Jesus stated that we are to be the salt of the earth and the light of the world. This means influencing the marketplace positively, standing out through our conduct and values, implementing fair business practices and policies that uphold ethical standards, and being a role model of integrity and inspiring your colleagues and employees to do the same.

An understanding of our position as kings means we carry a Kingdom mindset. We are not just working for earthly success, but for the advancement of God's Kingdom. With this mindset, we can envision and work toward transforming the marketplace, ensuring that business practices align with Kingdom values: **"This message is most trustworthy, and concerning these things I want you to insist steadfastly, so that those who have believed in (trusted in, relied on) God may be careful to apply themselves to honorable occupations and to doing good, for such things are [not only] excellent and right [in themselves], but [they are] good and profitable for the people" (Tit. 3:8 AMPC).** In your position as the righteous, you should develop business strategies that not only seek profit but also contribute to societal well-being and justice, and use your platform to support and uplift those in need, reflecting Christ's love and compassion.

Understanding your position in Christ as a Christian is crucial. It provides the foundation for you to reign in life, which includes the marketplace. You are not just another player in the business world; you are an ambassador of God's Kingdom, equipped with grace and righteousness to make a difference. Approach your work with confidence, integrity, and a vision of transformation, knowing you carry the authority and favor of Christ with you. By grounding yourself in these truths, you'll not only find personal fulfillment but also witness the incredible ways God can work through you to impact the marketplace for His glory.

The last place we will discuss that salvation being restored is in personage. Personage is defined as a person of rank, note, or distinction. **"This means that anyone who belongs to Christ has become a new person. The old life is gone; a new life has begun" (II Cor. 5:17 NLT)!** As Believers, our old self, with its prior motivations and behaviors, has been transformed. We are now new creations in Christ, with a renewed identity and purpose. Our new identity in Christ should be evident in the marketplace through our integrity and moral character. We uphold standards of honesty, truthfulness, and reliability, distinguishing ourselves from practices that compromise these values. **"In everything, set them an example by doing what is good. In your teaching, show integrity, seriousness, and soundness of speech that cannot be condemned, so that those who oppose you may be ashamed because they have nothing bad to say about us" (Tit. 2:7-8 NIV).** We present ourselves authentically, without resorting to deceit or manipulation. This authenticity fosters trust and respect in professional relationships. Being a new creation means we view the world, and our work, through a godly perspective. We prioritize values and principles that align with God's will. Our approach to the work environment is from God's perspective. This means that our work is driven by a higher purpose—to glorify God and serve others. This purpose enriches our work and inspires those around us.

As new creatures in Christ, we function with a renewed mind that proves, lives out, and brandishes God's good, acceptable, and perfect will. A renewed mind brings fresh, creative solutions and a vision for impact beyond profit. This can lead to innovative approaches that benefit both the business and the community. As new creations, we are guided and empowered by the Holy Spirit. This presence enables us to exhibit the fruit of the Spirit (Gal. 5:22-23) in our professional lives. We approach colleagues, clients, and competitors with love and compassion, building bridges and fostering positive relationships. We practice patience and self-control in high-pressure situations, setting an example of grace under pressure.

Agents of Reconciliation

All this is from God, who reconciled us to Himself through Christ and gave us the ministry of reconciliation: that God was reconciling the world to Himself in Christ, not counting people's sins against them. And He has committed to us the message of reconciliation.
—II Corinthians 5:18-19 NIV

Second Corinthians 5:18-19 speaks about how we have been given the ministry of reconciliation. Reconciliation involves restoring man from our broken relationship with God through Christ. But this is not where it stops. Reconciliation is also the assignment of restoring to God's servants—Believers—the stewardship of what we forfeited to Satan in the fall of Adam.

Because we only view our jobs as work and not mission, we take an unbalanced approach to our purpose for being there. In God's eyes, our job is His opportunity to win a soul, because a soul already won is in the field. We are commissioned to continue Christ's work of reconciliation, helping others find peace with God and with one another. Our lives should exemplify the reconciliation we preach, demonstrating love, forgiveness, and unity in our interactions.

> With a servant's heart you lead, investing in the growth and well-being of your team.

As new creations in Christ, our ministry of reconciliation should also be exemplary in the marketplace, aiming to reconcile and restore business relationships back under Kingdom governing. As agents of reconciliation, we actively seek to resolve conflicts rather than allow them to fester. This may involve mediating disputes, fostering open communication, and promoting understanding. God has equipped the Believer with Kingdom skills for conflict resolution: proactively seeking to resolve conflicts and promote peace, contributing to a harmonious work environment.

You have the ability to unite people around a common goal, no matter their gender or ethnicity. You lead inclusively, valuing each individual's unique contributions and creating a culture of mutual respect and collaboration: **"Let each of you esteem and look upon and be concerned for not [merely] his own interests, but also each for the interests of others" (Phil. 2:4 AMPC).** The new you leads with a different heart—a servant's heart. With a servant's heart, you lead by investing in the growth and well-being of your team. Your leadership style is characterized by humility, encouragement, and a focus on developing others, mirroring Christ's servant leadership. As a new creation, you prioritize ethical business practices. This might include fair trade, sustainable sourcing, and honest marketing. Your choices reflect a commitment to integrity and stewardship of God's creation.

Being a new creation also means recognizing the marketplace as a mission field. You recognize and value the diverse backgrounds and perspectives of team members and encourage inclusive practices that ensure every voice is heard and valued. Your decision-making process reflects your new identity in Christ. You seek God's wisdom through prayer and Scripture, ensuring that your choices align with Godly principles and contribute to long-term, righteous outcomes. Embracing your new identity in Christ transforms how you engage with the marketplace. You bring a different quality of person, one marked by integrity, vision, love, and reconciliation. Your presence becomes a testimony of God's transforming power and a beacon of light in the business world.

You are a change agent. The investment in you should bring a difference to the company. Companies known for their ethical and reconciliatory practices earn respect and loyalty from customers, employees, and partners. This leads to a stronger brand and better business outcomes; that's what you bring. Being an agent of reconciliation in the marketplace is a high calling that reflects Christ's mission. It involves living out the Gospel in practical ways, fostering peace, understanding, and ethical standards in a world often driven by conflict and self-interest. Remember, each act of reconciliation not only builds immediate relationships but also sows seeds of God's Kingdom, bringing hope and transformation to the broader community.

Walking with God in Business

The Lord detests dishonest scales, but accurate weights find favor with Him.
—**Proverbs 11:1NIV**

I ran a very successful barbershop for a number of years before I was called to go into ministry full-time. I received several awards, was recognized by the city, and was one of the only shops during that time running a commercial on television. The shop was clean and well-maintained, and my staff knew my rules. I was told that I could not run a successful Christian barbershop. But Jireh's Cuts became a staple shop in the hair care community. The point is, I did not have to sit God to the side in order to have an effective business. As a matter fact, I attribute my huge impact with this business to my relationship with God and the business biblical principles. The business market is only absent of God because many don't take God with them, though they pray that He increases them there. I never saw sitting God to the side as an option. Instead, I saw God as my business partner. **"We then, as workers together with Him" (I Cor. 6:1a)**. Years after I left that industry, people were still inquiring about whether or not I would come back. The point I'm conveying is that God is committed to the success of the sum total of your life.

Your personal walk with God shouldn't be across the street from your relationship with him in your profession. Many Christian businesspeople choose to separate their relationship with God from their business, but trusting in God and living for God means that He is incorporated in all of your life, and you rely on His wisdom and guidance in all decisions, including your business, rather than isolating Him solely to your personal life. Believers lack a given advantage when they do business on the basis of human understanding and logic only. Biblical principles should be incorporated in strategic planning sessions, leadership training, and workflow, and God should be invited to direct the vision and mission of the business.

The character of God in your business model is not something that is dismissive and uninviting to the marketplace. God values honesty and fairness in all dealings: **"The Lord detests dishonest scales" (Prov. 11 NIV).** When the aforementioned scripture is applied directly to business transactions, it ensures that all parties are treated justly. With God as our business partner, when tempted to cut corners or engage in questionable practices, seeking God's guidance can strengthen our resolve to act with integrity. The scripture encourages Believers to approach their work with the highest level of dedication and excellence, viewing their efforts as service to God: **"Whatever you do, work at it with all your heart, as working for the Lord, not for human masters, since you know that you will receive an inheritance from the Lord as a reward. It is the Lord Christ you are serving" (Col. 3:23-24).**

There should be a notable difference when a person encounters a Kingdom citizen in the marketplace—a level of excellence in all aspects of business, from product quality to customer interactions and performance. Believers recognize doing business as a high level of responsibility and stewardship because it's viewed as an act of worship and service to God. Faith doesn't just work in our private lives. Faith works in the marketplace. The Scripture calls Believers not just to hear the Word but also to act on it. This means applying biblical principles actively and consistently in all areas of life, including business: **"But be ye doers of the word, and not hearers only, deceiving your own selves" (James 1:22).** You can implement practical actions that exemplify biblical teachings, such as fairness, honesty, and compassion, in everyday business operations. Begin each workday with prayer and meditation on scripture, seeking God's wisdom for the tasks ahead. Use the Bible as a foundation for developing business policies and practices, ensuring alignment with God's principles. Let integrity be your witness. Conduct business in a way that reflects Christ's love and integrity, serving as a testimony to colleagues, clients, and competitors.

I believe that the marketplace is the perfect place for the working of the Word. It is what gives the Believer the overwhelming advantage: **"Then all the peoples on earth will see that you are called by the name of the Lord, and they will fear you" (Deut. 28:10 NIV).** When Believers live and operate according to God's Word, His presence and favor become evident to others. This then distinguishes you from others and serves as a witness of God's goodness to His people: **"Then the disciples went out and preached everywhere, and the Lord worked with them and confirmed his word by the signs that accompanied it" (Mark 16:20 NIV).** When non-Believers observe the uncompromising integrity and excellence with which Believers conduct business, it sets a powerful example. From transparent dealings to fair labor practices, ethical standards grounded in God's Word show non-Believers a different and higher standard. Delivering high-quality work and going the extra mile reflect God's character, drawing respect and admiration from others.

> The business market is only absent of God because many don't take God with them.

When the Word is lived out in the daily affairs of life, the Believer embodies principles of peace and reconciliation in resolving conflicts, and this profoundly influences those who witness it. You are a living testimony of God's work. This often leads non-Believers to inquire more about the faith and sometimes even leads to their conversions. Integrating biblical principles helps build a positive organizational culture that attracts talent and helps retain employees. Employees in organizations that operate by biblical principles often report higher job satisfaction, engagement, and morale.

There is also a benefit to you as well. A biblical approach to work can encourage a healthier work-life balance, avoiding the pitfalls of burnout and stress. Operating with a sense of divine purpose in business brings deeper fulfillment and motivation. The Word of God is not just for the church or personal life; it has profound power and relevance in the marketplace. By living out the principles of scripture in business, Believers can make a positive impact on others' lives, serve as powerful witnesses to non-Believers, and enjoy God's favor and blessings.

By embodying God's Word in your business practices, you are setting yourself apart, bringing light into the business world, and providing a compelling testament to the transformative power of walking with God.

Chapter 2
The Convergence of Business and Ministry

Make it your goal to live a quiet life, minding your own business and working with your hands, just as we instructed you before. Then people who are not Believers will respect the way you live, and you will not need to depend on others.
—I Thessalonians 4:11-12

In the life of a Believer, there is no separation between ministry and business. Both serve a common purpose—the expansion of God's Kingdom on earth. The marketplace, where business, trade, and economics intersect, plays a critical role in advancing God's Kingdom agenda. It is not just a space for transactions or profit, but a mission field where the principles of heaven can be replicated on earth. The decisions made in the marketplace have a profound impact on the economy, the direction of society, and, ultimately, the personal lives of people. This is why the Kingdom of God is needed in the marketplace: it affects every aspect of life, including the home, family, and community.

For the Believer, business is not merely a means to make a living; it is a platform for Kingdom influence. The marketplace is one of the most powerful engines driving the economy, and its influence reaches into every area of society. Decisions made by businesses affect employment, resource distribution, and even the moral and ethical climate of nations. When Believers engage in business with a Kingdom mindset, they become agents of transformation, bringing God's values of justice, integrity, stewardship, and generosity into a space that impacts millions of lives. Proverbs 11:10 TLB says, **"The whole city celebrates a good man's success—and also the godless man's death brings cheers."** This scripture emphasizes the far-reaching impact of leadership in the marketplace. A righteous person's success is not confined to personal gain; it brings prosperity and blessing to entire communities. When Kingdom principles are applied in business, they ripple out, influencing the economy and elevating the quality of life for people.

Similarly, Matthew 5:13 NCV says, **"You are the salt of the earth. But if the salt loses its salty taste, it cannot be made salty again. It is good for nothing, except to be thrown out and walked on."** This passage speaks to the Believer's role in the world, particularly in the marketplace. Just as salt preserves and enhances, Believers are called to preserve what is good and enhance society by injecting the values of the Kingdom into their work. If the marketplace lacks the influence of the Kingdom, it becomes subject to corruption, greed, and moral decay, which then impacts the economy and the personal lives of individuals.

The marketplace is the engine that drives the economy. Decisions made by businesses, industries, and entrepreneurs affect the direction of the economy—what goods are produced, how wealth is distributed, and what resources are available to families. When the marketplace operates without Kingdom values, it often leads to economic disparity, exploitation, and greed. But when Believers bring the Kingdom of God into the marketplace, the economic landscape can be transformed to reflect God's principles of fairness, provision, and stewardship.

Deuteronomy 8:18 (NCV) says, **"But remember the Lord your God! It is he who gives you the power to become rich, keeping the agreement he promised to your ancestors, as it is today."**

This passage reveals that wealth creation is a part of God's covenant with His people. The ability to generate wealth and influence the economy is a divine gift meant to establish His Kingdom on earth. When Believers understand this, they see their role in the marketplace as more than business transactions—they see it as a way to bring Kingdom principles into the economy and positively affect the direction of nations.

Moreover, when Kingdom values govern the marketplace, it promotes ethical business practices, fair wages, and a just economic system that uplifts families and communities. Proverbs 21:5 TLB says, **"Steady plodding brings prosperity; hasty speculation brings poverty."** This verse reinforces the idea that Kingdom principles in business, diligence, integrity, and patience—lead to economic stability and prosperity, which benefits not just the business owner but society at large.

The decisions made in the marketplace don't just affect the economy; they ripple into the personal lives of people. The marketplace shapes the jobs people hold, the wages they earn, the products they can afford, and the quality of life they experience. A marketplace governed by Kingdom principles provides stability, security, and fairness, allowing families to thrive, **"Good people leave their wealth to their grandchildren, but a sinner's wealth is stored up for good people" (Prov. 13:22 NCV).** This scripture highlights the generational impact of righteous decisions in the marketplace. When Believers operate businesses or lead organizations with a Kingdom mindset, they are not just building wealth for themselves, but they are creating a legacy of provision that blesses their children, grandchildren, and entire communities.

Furthermore, the marketplace's role in shaping the economy impacts the home. When wages are fair, families can provide for their needs, and children can grow up in secure environments. Conversely, when the marketplace is driven by greed and corruption, it leads to economic instability, poverty, and broken homes. This is why it is crucial for Believers to step into the marketplace and operate with the principles of God's Kingdom, ensuring that the wealth and resources generated there contribute to the well-being of families and society, **"All goes well for the generous man who conducts his business fairly" (Psalm 112:5 TLB)**. When Kingdom-minded people engage in business with generosity and fairness, it creates an environment of blessing that impacts not only the business but the personal lives of everyone involved. Fair business practices lead to equitable distribution of wealth and resources, which ultimately strengthens families and communities.

The Kingdom of God is not limited to church walls or personal spirituality. It is meant to permeate every aspect of life, including the marketplace. The marketplace plays a pivotal role in shaping the economy and influencing personal lives, which is why it is essential for Believers to bring Kingdom values into business and commerce. By doing so, they contribute to the expansion of God's Kingdom on earth, creating a ripple effect that touches the economy, strengthens families, and replicates heaven's principles in the marketplace, **"Let your Kingdom come and let your will be done on earth as it is done in heaven"** (Matt. 6:10 NCV). This prayer encompasses every area of life, including the marketplace. It is a call for Believers to bring the values of the Kingdom into their work, businesses, and economic systems, ensuring that God's will is done in every transaction, every job, and every decision that impacts the world.

The marketplace plays a crucial role in shaping the economy and the personal lives of people, and when Believers engage the marketplace with a Kingdom mindset, they have the power to bring about economic justice, generational prosperity, and societal transformation. By operating with diligence, integrity, and generosity, Kingdom entrepreneurs and business leaders not only succeed but also create environments that replicate heaven's principles on earth, influencing both the economy and the lives of countless individuals.

The Bible in Your Business

In today's fast-paced business world, corporations are constantly looking for innovative ways to increase their bottom line. What many people may not realize is that some of the most successful companies are unknowingly applying principles that can be traced directly back to the Bible. These companies, whether knowingly or unknowingly, are tapping into timeless wisdom that has guided successful enterprises for centuries. Meanwhile, many Christian business owners and professionals are missing out on applying these same biblical principles to their own ventures. The Bible is full of wisdom that, when applied to business, can bring sustainable success and integrity to any organization. The scripture above provides a profound blueprint for business conduct for the Believer. This means we know exactly what is required for success in business, as II Peter 1:3 says, **"According as His divine power hath given unto us all things that pertain <u>unto life</u> and godliness, through the knowledge of Him that hath called us to glory and virtue."** We will come back to this later.

At first glance, the passage in I Thessalonians may seem to be focused on individual conduct, but when we dig deeper, it reveals critical principles that can be applied directly to business. The instruction to "do your own business" and "work with your own hands" encourages a disciplined approach to work and enterprise, where personal responsibility and diligence are central. The result of this, according to verse 12, is that Believers will be able to "walk honestly" and experience no lack. These foundational principles of diligence, personal responsibility, and integrity are key elements of any successful business.

Many of the world's most successful companies are built on principles that align with biblical teachings, even though they may not explicitly acknowledge them. There are some companies that are known for integrating Christian values into their business models, but even secular companies like Google, Amazon, and Apple incorporate practices that reflect biblical wisdom. For example, one of the key principles in the Bible is stewardship, which involves managing resources wisely. Proverbs 21:5 says, **"The plans of the diligent lead surely to plenty, but those of everyone who is hasty, surely to poverty."** This principle of careful planning, diligence, and resource management is a major reason why companies like Amazon have succeeded. Amazon's focus on operational efficiency, customer service, and long-term growth reflects a commitment to stewardship, ensuring that every resource, from employee hours to logistical processes, is used effectively. Excellence is a biblical value found in scripture and reflected in successful businesses. Businesses like Tesla and Google thrive by pursuing excellence in innovation, constantly pushing the boundaries of what is possible in their industries. The drive for excellence leads to increased value in the marketplace, better products, and long-term success.

While secular companies are benefiting from these biblical principles, many Christian business owners and professionals are missing out on the same opportunities because they aren't applying the wisdom of the Word in their own enterprises: **"And the lord commended the unjust steward, because he had done wisely: for the children of this world are in their generation wiser than the children of light" (Luke 16:8).** There is often a disconnect between faith and work, where Believers may compartmentalize their spiritual life and their business life, failing to see how closely the two are intertwined. The Bible is not just a spiritual guidebook; it is also a practical manual for how to live and work in the world. The principles found in scripture are universal and apply to every aspect of life, including business. Unfortunately, many Believers fail to realize that the same Bible they read for spiritual growth also contains the wisdom they need to excel in their professional lives.

The principles found in scripture are universal and apply to every aspect of life, including business.

In today's competitive marketplace, Christian businessmen and women have the opportunity to stand out by applying biblical principles in their businesses. However, when Believers fail to integrate these principles into their business models, they miss out on the favor, growth, and sustainability that God promises to those who follow His ways. For instance, the principle of *diligence* is central to both personal and business success. Yet, many Christian professionals may overlook this in favor of seeking shortcuts or quick profits. The Bible consistently emphasizes the value of hard work and perseverance. Proverbs 12:24 says, **"The hand of the diligent shall bear rule: but the slothful shall be under tribute."** Diligence in business, whether it's careful financial management, attention to customer service, or developing a long-term vision, leads to stability and prosperity. When Christians neglect this, they often find themselves struggling, even as others thrive.

Another missed opportunity is the practice of integrity. While some Believers operate with honesty and fairness, others may be tempted to compromise their values to stay competitive. But the Word is clear: integrity brings long-term blessings. Proverbs 10:9 says, **"He that walketh uprightly walketh surely: but he that perverteth his ways shall be known."** Trust is one of the most valuable assets in business, and when Christians commit to maintaining integrity in all their dealings, they position themselves for success, just as secular businesses that value transparency have done. This is the most important thing to me. I keep it in the forefront of all that I do, because Proverbs 11:3 says, **"The integrity of the upright shall guide them: but the perverseness of transgressors shall destroy them."**

There is also the biblical principle of service. This principle is often underutilized by Christian business leaders. Jesus modeled servant leadership, and businesses that adopt this mindset stand out in a crowded marketplace. Matthew 20:26 says, **"But it shall not be so among you: but whosoever will be great among you, let him be your minister."** Service-oriented companies such as Zappos, which prioritizes customer satisfaction, and Southwest Airlines, which focuses on employee happiness, have thrived because they value serving others. Believers have the same opportunity to demonstrate Christ-like service in their businesses, showing the world what it looks like to lead with a heart for others. If we are to model the image of Christ, it should be done in all arenas of life. It is the principle of service that gets a person to the top, **"But they held their peace: for by the way they had disputed among themselves, who should be the greatest. And He sat down, and called the twelve, and saith unto them, If any man desire to be first, the same shall be last of all, and servant of all" (Mark 9:34-35).**

A Biblical Business Model

There is business wisdom to be unlocked in the Word. The challenge for Christian business leaders is not merely recognizing that the Bible contains valuable wisdom for business, but learning how to apply these principles practically. As Christians, we have access to the greatest source of wisdom, and it's time we use it to shape the way we do business, bringing the values of the Kingdom into the marketplace for the glory of God and the benefit of others. If you want to see your business stand out from the others, here are several ways to begin integrating biblical principles into your business model:

1. **Build a foundation of integrity**—Integrity is the cornerstone of long-term success. Ensure that your business practices are transparent, fair, and ethical. This builds trust with clients, employees, and partners. As Proverbs 22:1 says, **"A good name is rather to be chosen than great riches."** Building a strong reputation through integrity is more valuable than short-term gains.

2. **Pursue excellence in all areas**—Don't settle for mediocrity in any aspect of your business. Commit to doing your work with excellence, whether it's the quality of your product, the level of customer service, or the way you manage your team. Ecclesiastes 9:10 says, **"Whatsoever thy hand findeth to do, do it with thy might."** Excellence attracts success and sets you apart in a competitive marketplace.

3. **Apply diligence in stewardship**—Stewardship is about managing resources wisely. Take time to create sound financial practices, manage your time effectively, and invest in long-term strategies rather than quick fixes. **Luke 16:10** reminds us, "He that is faithful in that which is least is faithful also in much." Diligence in small areas builds the capacity for larger successes.

4. **Lead with a heart of service**—Make serving others the heart of your business. Whether it's serving your customers, employees, or community, following the model of servant leadership creates a culture of care that resonates with people. As Jesus demonstrated, true leadership comes through service.

For Believers, the opportunity to integrate biblical wisdom into our business models is not just an option but a responsibility. By aligning our business practices with the principles found in scripture, we not only honor God, but we position ourselves for success that is sustainable, ethical, and impactful.

Life Includes Business

Back to II Peter 1:2-3, "According as His divine power hath given unto us **all things that pertain unto life** <u>and godliness</u>, through the knowledge of Him that hath called us to glory and virtue." This verse is a powerful reminder that God, in His divine power, has given Believers everything they need for both life and godliness. However, many people overlook the full scope of what this verse entails, especially the fact that "life" includes every area of our existence, including business, financial decisions, and making wise deals. Too often, Christians compartmentalize their faith, seeing the Bible as a spiritual guidebook for godliness but not as a practical manual for life, including how to operate in the marketplace. When Peter speaks about God providing "all things that pertain unto life," he isn't limiting the concept of life to spiritual matters alone. "Life" here encompasses all aspects of human existence: our relationships, work, decisions, finances, and, yes, even

> The Bible isn't a book of just "spiritual" virtues but practical keys to business

business. This means that the Bible offers wisdom for every situation we face, not just in personal relationships or moral behavior, but also in business dealings, leadership, and entrepreneurship.

The tendency to overlook this comprehensive application often leads to a disconnect between faith and practical living. Many Christians are unaware that the Bible contains principles that directly apply to business—principles about how to treat employees, manage finances, make ethical decisions, and negotiate deals with integrity. When we separate our faith from these areas of life, we fail to tap into the divine wisdom that God has already provided for us. If the Bible tells us how to treat our enemies, handle animals, train our children, deal with our money, and many other areas of life, why would it leave out the one thing that we all are a part of that provides resources, and the place where we live out purpose—in business? This is where the Church lacked teaching the difference between the Church as an institution versus the Church as an organism, so that when we go to the Word, our minds can see the business implications it provides.

However, the Bible is, in fact, a business manual. Proverbs 3:5-6 tells us, **"Trust in the Lord with all your heart and lean not on your own understanding; <u>in all your ways</u> acknowledge Him, and He will direct your paths."** This is a foundational principle for business. Trusting in God's wisdom rather than relying solely on human logic can lead to decisions that are both profitable and ethical. By acknowledging God in our business dealings, we position ourselves to receive divine insight and favor. The Bible isn't a book of just "spiritual" virtues, but practical keys to business success. God's Word is not just about moral living, but about making wise decisions in all areas of life, including business deals. James 1:5 reminds us, **"If any of you lack wisdom, let him ask of God, that giveth to all men liberally, and upbraideth not; and it shall be given him."** This wisdom also applies to how we negotiate, invest, and manage our finances.

The Bible is full of practical advice that helps Believers avoid the pitfalls of greed, deceit, and impulsive decision-making in business. Many people view the Bible as strictly a religious book, focused on spiritual teachings and moral guidance. While this is true, the Bible is also filled with profound wisdom and principles that apply directly to business. It contains stories of entrepreneurs, leaders, and individuals who made an impact in their world through trade, governance, and innovation. When examined closely, it becomes clear that the Bible is not just a book about worship, but also about how to navigate the complexities of life, including the world of business. The scripture provides a roadmap for wise financial stewardship, encouraging Believers to seek counsel, avoid debt when possible, and invest in ways that are sustainable and ethical: **"The plans of the diligent lead surely to plenty, but those of everyone who is hasty, surely to poverty" (Prov. 21:5)**. In business, this means taking time to plan wisely, making calculated decisions, and avoiding impulsive actions.

Do you want to build? Luke 14:28 tells us, **"For which of you, intending to build a tower, sitteth not down first, and counteth the cost, whether he have sufficient to finish it?"** This is a principle of planning and foresight that directly applies to business. Before making significant investments or entering into deals, we are called to count the cost, ensuring that our decisions are well thought out and aligned with God's wisdom. This kind of foresight helps Believers make business decisions that lead to long-term success rather than short-term gains.

When we fully embrace the truth of 2 Peter 1:3—that God has given us all we need for both life and godliness—we realize that the Word of God is not limited to "spiritual" matters. It is a source of wisdom, guidance, and principles for every area of our lives, including business. The Bible equips us with what we need to succeed in the marketplace, to make wise deals, and to operate in integrity. By applying the Word of God to our businesses and financial decisions, we unlock the full potential of the wisdom God has given us for life.

Too often, Believers miss out on the abundance of wisdom the Bible offers for business because they don't recognize that it is relevant to their work. But when we bring our faith into every area of life, including our professional endeavors, we position ourselves to experience God's favor, guidance, and provision in every decision we make.

The Bible is more than a spiritual guide; it is a comprehensive manual for successful living, including in the world of business. Its principles of stewardship, leadership, integrity, generosity, and innovation apply directly to how we conduct business today. When approached with this understanding, the Bible offers a blueprint for achieving success while honoring God and making a positive impact in the marketplace. By following its teachings, Believers can operate as Kingdom-preneurs, bringing God's values into the world and advancing His agenda through their work.

For Christian business professionals, the marketplace represents a vital mission field where they can bring the values of God's Kingdom to bear on the world of commerce. The integration of Kingdom principles into business not only transforms the marketplace itself but also has far-reaching effects on society as a whole, impacting homes, communities, and nations. At its core, business reflects the values of those who lead and operate within it. When the marketplace is driven by secular values, such as profit at any cost, it often leads to unethical behavior, inequality, and exploitation. Corporations that prioritize short-term gains over long-term sustainability may cut corners, harm the environment, or underpay workers, all of which ultimately lead to broken systems and suffering communities. However, when Kingdom values are brought into the marketplace, the priorities shift. Kingdom-minded business professionals understand that success is not just about personal gain, but about stewardship, responsibility, and service to others. The marketplace becomes a platform for serving the greater good, aligning with the biblical commandment to **"love your neighbor as yourself" (Mark 12:31 NCV).** By upholding the values of integrity, fairness, generosity, and justice, Christian business professionals can transform the marketplace from a place of self-interest to one of service and stewardship.

God's interest in business is not limited to spiritual matters, but extends to the practical dealings of trade, commerce, and contracts: **"The Lord wants honest scales and balances; he wants all business agreements to be fair" (Prov. 16:11 NCV)**. The economy is not just an abstract concept—it is a reflection of the values that drive the marketplace. When the Kingdom of God is present in the marketplace, the economy begins to reflect the justice, fairness, and generosity central to God's character. This can be seen in how wealth is distributed, resources are managed, and opportunities are created.

When Kingdom-minded leaders influence the economy, they challenge the systems that perpetuate inequality and injustice: **"A man who gains by oppressing the poor or by bribing the rich shall end in poverty" (Prov. 22:16 TLB).** This verse illustrates how unjust economic practices lead to ruin, both for individuals and entire societies. In contrast, businesses that operate with Kingdom values create systems of equitable wealth distribution, where the poor are not exploited and where resources are used to uplift communities rather than concentrate wealth in the hands of a few.

As Christian business leaders embrace their role in the economy, they contribute to creating an economic system that reflects **God's Kingdom of abundance** rather than scarcity. This kind of economy fosters innovation, creates jobs, and promotes a culture of generosity, where businesses not only generate wealth but also use that wealth to invest in people, communities, and the environment.

For Christian business professionals, the call is clear: **business and ministry are not separate realms.** Your work in the marketplace is as much a part of your calling as your involvement in ministry. In fact, the marketplace may be one of the most powerful mission fields you will ever enter. By applying Kingdom principles in your business, you are actively expanding God's Kingdom on earth and influencing the world for His glory. Every transaction, every decision, every interaction is an opportunity to serve God and to manifest His Kingdom on earth. By working with excellence, integrity, and a heart for service, you bring the light of the Kingdom into the marketplace, transforming the economy, communities, and personal lives in the process.

Chapter 3
The "In Particular"

For we are God's handiwork, created in Christ Jesus to do good works, which God prepared in advance for us to do.
—Ephesians 2:10 NIV

You have been given authority and power. You have something that is distinct and different, and you are intricately made by God with a specific purpose and set of gifts. Something "in particular;" **uniquely exclusive** to who and what God has called you to do in the earth. It is tailored to fit you: **"For we are God's handiwork, created in Christ Jesus to do good works, which God prepared in advance for us to do" (Eph. 2:10 NIV)**. You are created intentionally for good works and the unique contributions that you are meant to make in the world.

The majority of people overlook that thing that makes them different and sets them apart from others, not knowing that that is the very thing that God gifted them with to thrive. There is a certain faith, confidence, and determination that comes with recognizing that God has known and set us apart for a specific purpose: **"Before I formed you in the womb I knew you, before you were born I set you apart; I appointed you as a prophet to the nations" (Jer. 1:5 NIV).** Believing in your unique purpose and acting on it are both essential to fulfilling the good works God has prepared for you. biblical characters like Moses, Esther, and David demonstrate that trusting in God's design, overcoming self-doubt, and taking faithful action lead to fulfilling one's unique purpose and making a significant impact.

God-given abilities, or what I refer to as the "in particular," are far more than natural talents or learned skills; they are the unique capacities God has placed within each person, designed for a divine purpose. These abilities are not limited by human expectations, circumstances, or the world's definitions of success. When someone taps into their "in particular," they are operating with a supernatural advantage, empowered by God to impact their sphere of influence in ways that transcend human logic or societal limitations. **"As for these four youths, God gave them learning and skill in all literature and wisdom, and Daniel had understanding in all visions and dreams. And in every matter of wisdom and understanding about which the king inquired of them, he found them ten times better than all the magicians and enchanters that were in all his kingdom (Dan. 1:17,20 ESV).**

You are authorized, licensed, qualified, permitted, and equipped to do something.

The capacity of a God-given ability is vast because it originates from an infinite source—God Himself. For instance, Joseph's ability to interpret dreams didn't just give him insight; it opened doors for him in the highest levels of Egyptian society, placing him in a position of leadership. His capacity was enlarged as he trusted God through trials and setbacks. What began as a simple ability in a prison cell became a tool to save nations during a famine (Genesis 41:15-16). This highlights that our "in particular" often starts in small, unnoticed places but has the potential to grow beyond our imagination when we submit it to God. The beauty of these abilities is that they are tailor-made for each individual's calling.

When the "in particular" is embraced, it opens up vast possibilities in the Kingdom of God. Joseph is a prime example of this truth. Though he was betrayed by his brothers and sold into slavery, he trusted God and relied on his gift of interpreting dreams. This in-particular ability ultimately led him to a position of great influence, where he saved not only his family but the entire nation of Egypt (Gen. 50:20).

Another person is Ester. Her capacity to influence didn't lie in military strength or political power but in her ability to act with wisdom, courage, and favor. Her "in particular" was relational influence, which became a critical asset at the right time. God positioned her uniquely so that, in a single moment of obedience, she could save an entire nation (Esther 4:14).

David's God-given capacity began with shepherding sheep, but when combined with his faith in God, it enabled him to conquer a giant warrior that the entire army of Israel feared. His in-particular ability to sling a stone accurately, paired with his trust in God, expanded beyond the field into the battlefield and eventually into the kingdom. David's story teaches us that no ability is too small or insignificant when it is aligned with God's purpose (1 Sam. 17:45-47).

Peter, despite his failures, embodied a God-given boldness that allowed him to speak with authority and lead thousands to Christ in the early Church. His "in particular" was his raw, fearless proclamation of the gospel, even in the face of persecution. God used Peter's personality, imperfections, and ability to lead with passion, showing us that our God-given abilities can work through our weaknesses and transform us into vessels of His power (Acts 2:14).

What makes these abilities so powerful is their source: Holy Spirit. Romans 12:6-8 tells us that we each have **different gifts according to the grace God has given us**. This means that our abilities are not only unique but also empowered by divine grace. This grace is what enables a person to go beyond their natural limitations. It's the same grace that allowed Moses, a man with a stutter, to confront Pharaoh and lead an entire nation out of slavery. His capacity was not determined by his natural ability but by the God who empowered him. When someone operates in their "in particular," they are stepping into the limitless potential that God has woven into their destiny. As Ephesians 3:20 reminds us, God is able to do "immeasurably more than all we ask or imagine, according to his power that is at work within us." The power at work within us is directly tied to our "in particular." As we trust God, cultivate our gifts, and allow Him to stretch our capacity, there are no limits to what we can accomplish for the Kingdom.

In the marketplace, this means that when we walk confidently in our God-given abilities, we are not only equipped to succeed but also to bring Kingdom influence into every sector of society. Whether in business, education, arts, government, or ministry, our "in particular" has the capacity to change atmospheres, solve problems, and bring hope to a world that desperately needs it. By recognizing and embracing the vast potential of our God-given abilities, we can fully step into our purpose and see God use us in extraordinary ways.

Many times, the misfortune of a person's life can overshadow their good works and even the purpose for which they were called. This is the case with Samson. People forget that he was called of God, and that the Spirit of God even moved with him. Samson was the last judge of Israel. His assignment was to begin to deliver Israel out of the hands of the Philistines (Judges 13:5). God gave Samson special, supernatural strength. He killed a thousand men alone, caught three hundred foxes, tore down gates to a city, and carried them off singlehandedly. This wasn't Samson's doing alone. Samson did this operating in his "in particular." See, Samson was made for it. All of the things previously mentioned were done to the Philistines, the people that he was appointed and anointed to judge. He always saw success when he operated in his "in particular." Nothing the Philistines did could defeat him.

The Philistines came up with a plan. They used Samson's own people, the Israelites, to catch him. Knowing that they did not have the ability to do so, they threatened his, people who agreed out of fear. I think this part of the story is worth reading:

> And the men of Judah said, Why are ye come up against us? And they answered, To bind Samson are we come up, to do to him as he hath done to us. Then three thousand men of Judah went to

> the top of the rock Etam, and said to Samson, Knowest thou not that the Philistines are rulers over us? What is this that thou hast done unto us? And he said unto them, As they did unto me, so have I done unto them. And they said unto him, We are come down to bind thee, that we may deliver thee into the hand of the Philistines. And Samson said unto them, Swear unto me, that ye will not fall upon me yourselves. And they spake unto him, saying, No; but we will bind thee fast, and deliver thee into their hand: but surely we will not kill thee. And they bound him with two new cords, and brought him up from the rock. And when he came unto Lehi, the Philistines shouted against him: and the Spirit of the Lord came mightily upon him, and the cords that were upon his arms became as flax that was burnt with fire, and his bands loosed from off his hands. And he found a new jawbone of an ass, and put forth his hand, and took it, and slew a thousand men therewith. [1]And Samson said, With the jawbone of an ass, heaps upon heaps, with the jaw of an ass have I slain a thousand men. And it came to pass, when he had made an end of speaking, that he cast away the jawbone out of his hand, and called that place Ramath-lehi (Judges 15:10-17).

What I wanted you to see in the story is how Samson's "in particular" did not work against his own people. They were able to bound him—a man who tore a lion apart and carried city gates—with two cords. It is possible that the easiest things become the most difficult for us because they are outside of the wheelhouse of our anointing.

You are anointed for something and not everything. Samson's strength only worked when he was up against the Philistines, because that is the place and people that he was assigned to. Once in the presence of his assignment, the Bible says that the cords that were upon his arms became as flax that was burnt with fire, and his bands loosed from off his hands, and he defeated a thousand men with the jawbone of an ass.

I want this story to speak to you about the importance of your "in particular," that special thing that God has empowered you with. We often go through life searching for things to do rather than discovering the thing we were anointed to do. We would rather find the thing that will brand us as successful rather than get into the thing that God purposed to make us great.

You are empowered for something "in particular." Instead of trying to be a master at all things, first discover the one thing that God divinely purposed and gifted you in. There is something that you have already been perfected at. It just has to be discovered and then stirred up: **"This is why I remind you to (stir up) <u>fan into flames</u> the spiritual gift God gave you when I laid my hands on you. For God has not given us a spirit of fear and timidity, but of power, love, and self-discipline (II Tim. 1:6-7 NLT).** Don't allow the greatest part of you to lie dormant any longer. We can't afford to be doing things outside of what we have been called, sent, and assigned to do—not everything we do gets God's backing. The one thing that already has God's backing is the "in particular:" **"Before I formed you in the womb I knew you, and before you were born I consecrated you; I appointed you a prophet to the nations" (Jer. 1:5 ESV).**

Wealthy Already

When you understand this, your entire approach to the business market changes. You aren't making money—you're doing ministry. You are on an assignment. Most people go into the marketplace with a mind of how much money they intend to make, how to cut the best deal, how to get higher pay, or what it will take to move up the corporate ladder for a better position. And although there is nothing wrong with any of these, as a Kingdom citizen in the marketplace, the approach is wrong. You never go in empty-handed. You are His representative-source. You are the answer: **"So we are Christ's ambassadors, <u>God making His appeal as it were through us.</u> <u>We [as Christ's personal representatives]</u> beg you for His sake to lay hold of the divine favor [now offered you] and be reconciled to God" (II Cor. 5:20AMPC).**

I was reluctant to put this particular part in a book whose purpose to inform and embolden Believers to go and do business in the marketplace. It really takes a different mindset. You can't have a Sunday service mindset if you are going to "do great "and "go big" in marketplace ministry. Just in typing those two statements, I can hear the Church-minded person asking, "Where is Jesus in that?" I can see spiritual peril rise in the heart of the Believer who wants to believe for more but over time has been taught to believe that is tantamount to chasing fame. The reason is that for decades, wealth has been preached about in the Church as being evil, and if there is any attempt to do anything for money, the person is immediately considered to be a heretic and lover of money. Another reason is that there is this false humility that the Church has accepted. We have even been mistaught about what it means to be content. We don't read the books of the Bible in the context of where the Church was at that time compared to the government's rule. We do not have a grounded understanding of what the Church is, her earthly purpose, or what the Kingdom of God is. We will even read a text and, because of our mindset, totally dismiss what the person really said and what God did: **"And Jabez called on the God of Israel, saying, Oh that thou wouldest bless me indeed, and enlarge my coast, and that thine hand might be with me, and that thou wouldest keep me from evil, that it may not grieve me! And God granted him that which he requested (I Chron. 4:10).** The scripture did not say that God put this on his heart. Jabez asked, and God answered. And it was to bless him. God led the children of Israel out of Egypt with silver and gold. They spoiled Egypt. And God even said, "Put it on your children." We skip that and go straight to the golden calf.

> Wealth is something that comes out of you and not something that comes to you.

I want to take a moment and tell you, the reader, that you do not have to fear being wealthy. It's not money that ruins a person, it's their heart. If your heart is to do good, then with wealth, you will do good. But if your heart is to do evil, even with a little money, you will do evil. **"A good person produces good things from the treasury**

of a good heart, and an evil person produces evil things from the treasury of an evil heart. What you say flows from what is in your heart" (Luke 6:45 NLT). God has no problem with you being wealthy. **"Praise ye the Lord. Blessed is the man that feareth the Lord, that delighteth greatly in his commandments. His seed shall be mighty upon earth: the generation of the upright shall be blessed. Wealth and riches shall be in his house: and his righteousness endureth for ever (Ps. 112:1-3).** The key is to define and become resolute, knowing that the purpose of wealth is to glorify God, and your heart posture is to please God and keep Him first.

The foundation of this book comes from Luke 19:13, which tells us to **"occupy till the lord comes."** The word *occupy* means "to do business." Here is an important revelation: if you are told to occupy, that means you would have to be given what you need to occupy. This means that we are already resourced, and our going simply brings out of us what has already been put in. The servants in Luke had in hand what they needed to go into the workforce and fulfill the occupying command. They had in hand the ability to produce more.

Now let's see the outcome of the ones who went in with this understanding of being wealthy already. **"The first servant reported, 'Master, I invested your money <u>and made ten times the original amount</u>!' 'Well done!' the king exclaimed. 'You are a good servant. You have been faithful with the little I entrusted to you, so you will be governor of ten cities as your reward'"(Luke 19:16-17 NLT).** I want to suggest to you to give new meaning to wealth. That wealth is something that comes out of you and not something that comes to you. You are wealthy already.

With assignment comes everything you need in order to get it done, including the reward from having done it (Matt. 25:21). I don't believe Believers totally understand their new life in Christ—that God had your new life planned out for you before you accepted Christ. You are born into a finished work, **"and ye are complete in Him" (Col. 2:10a)**. Every part of your life was taken care of. Salvation is a whole life package, and in it, there's wealth. This is what allows us to go into the marketplace with boldness, assurance, tenacity, and drive. Money doesn't become our drive, but glorifying God.

You should not hear this as God not wanting your businesses or you to grow and flourish or that you shouldn't give attention to the business of business or have a focus on your productivity or advancements. All of the aforementioned are God's will and should unquestionably be prevalent in the business dealings of Believers. We need goals, benchmarks, and an aspiration of being prosperous and evolving. However, these things are not the main thing. The main thing is that you and I bring glory to God.

There are a plethora of businesses who present these absent of God. But to Believers, our lights shine so that **men see our good work and glory the Father which is in heaven** (Matt. 5:16). If it's wealth without God, then it's not wealth—it is just good work skills. God made wealth a part of our Covenant right so that we would not have to chase it, but so that we could keep our eyes on Him: **"Do not toil to acquire wealth; be discerning enough to desist. When your eyes light on it, it is gone, for suddenly it sprouts wings, flying like an eagle toward heaven (Prov. 23:4-5 ESV).**

If you can make this mental pivot, I promise you it will change how you see and do business. **You are a wealth creator.** You move with a different confidence and pace. When you go with this mindset, it cuts out the competition, calms the chaos, and centers God as your source. This is what it truly means to walk by faith—the belief that it's already done.

I want to make sure that I am clear. I am not saying that we don't negotiate the deal, that you aren't aiming for the highest reward, that you accept whatever comes. This has been the mindset of the Church for decades and has resulted in distrust and disdain for Christians in the workspace because a lack of character and good work ethic usually follows. I am saying that because you always bring your very best because of who you are representing, the return is always the best—and nothing less.

The Intersection of Faith and Innovation

In today's rapidly evolving marketplace, innovation is often seen as the driving force behind success. For the believer, however, the power of faith combined with innovation offers a unique advantage. By tapping into both, Believers can achieve success not only in their business endeavors but also in every area of life. At the heart of this approach is the understanding that faith in God allows us to access divine wisdom, which in turn fuels creativity and innovation. Proverbs 8:12 says, "I wisdom dwell with prudence, and **find out knowledge of witty inventions**." This verse reminds us that wisdom from God leads to innovative ideas, insights, and solutions that are beyond human capability. As Believers, when we walk in faith and seek God's wisdom, we open ourselves up to divine inspiration and creative breakthroughs that can lead to significant success in the marketplace.

Faith is the foundation of every Believer's journey, and when it comes to business and innovation, faith plays a critical role. Hebrews 11:1 defines faith as **"the substance of things hoped for, the evidence of things not seen."** Faith allows Believers to move forward with boldness and confidence, trusting that God will provide the ideas, strategies, and opportunities needed to succeed, even when they cannot yet see the full picture. Faith opens the door to divine revelation, which fuels innovation.

Throughout the Bible, we see examples of people who, by faith, received creative solutions that set them apart and allowed them to prosper. Noah built an ark based on divine instructions, a structure that had never existed before. Joseph was given wisdom from God to store food in preparation for a famine, an economic innovation that saved Egypt. These examples show that when Believers trust God for guidance, they receive innovative ideas that bring success and solve real-world problems. For modern-day Believers, faith positions us to be receptive to God's voice. As we walk in faith, we can ask God for innovative ideas that will differentiate us in our industries, give

> . . . the combination of faith and innovation is a powerful tool for success.

us a competitive edge, and ultimately lead to Kingdom advancement. James 1:5 says, **"If any of you lack wisdom, let him ask of God, that giveth to all men liberally, and upbraideth not; and it shall be given him."** This is a promise that if we seek wisdom from God, He will generously provide it, allowing us to tap into divine creativity.

Innovation is a result of wisdom. Proverbs 8:12 is clear: wisdom leads to innovation. The phrase **"witty inventions"** speaks to the creative ideas, solutions, and strategies that come from God's wisdom. When we rely on God's wisdom, we unlock a level of insight that leads to innovation beyond what we can produce through human effort alone. Innovation is not limited to technology or product development. It includes finding new ways to solve problems, improve processes, and create value in the marketplace. When Believers tap into the wisdom of God, they are positioned to create innovative solutions that transform industries and open new doors of opportunity.

Consider the example of **George Washington Carver**, an inventor and scientist whose faith in God led to hundreds of innovative uses for the peanut, sweet potato, and other crops. Carver's brilliance wasn't simply the result of human intellect; he often credited his ideas to the divine inspiration he received during his morning prayer walks. Carver believed that by seeking God's wisdom, he could unlock the mysteries of nature and bring forth solutions that would benefit humanity. His faith fueled his innovation, and as a result, he became one of the most respected scientists of his time.

> Believers possess a unique ability to merge faith and innovations.

God is no respecter of persons. Believers today can rely on the wisdom of God to inspire innovation in their own fields. Whether it's in business, technology, education, or healthcare, the creative ideas that come from God's wisdom have the power to transform industries and create lasting success. For Christian entrepreneurs and business leaders, the combination of faith and innovation is a powerful tool for success. Faith allows you to step out boldly, trusting that God will guide you through the unknown, while innovation provides you with the fresh ideas and strategies needed to stay ahead in a competitive marketplace.

One of the keys to unlocking innovation is trusting God's timing and process. Innovation doesn't always happen overnight. It requires perseverance, trust, and, often, stepping out in faith without seeing the full plan. Isaiah 55:8-9 reminds us that God's ways are higher than our ways, and His thoughts higher than our thoughts. By faith, we must be willing to follow His lead, even when the path is unclear. Innovation, when driven by faith, is not about rushing to find quick solutions but about trusting that God's wisdom will reveal itself in due time. In practical terms, this means that Christian business leaders should incorporate faith into their innovation processes by seeking God in prayer, remaining open to divine guidance, and taking bold steps of faith when God provides an idea or insight. This reliance on God ensures that innovation is aligned with His purposes, leading not only to business success but also to Kingdom impact.

Faith and innovation go hand in hand in advancing the Kingdom of God in the marketplace. **Believers possess a unique ability to merge faith and innovations.** Remember, I have been saying throughout this entire book that the world needs answers. And they are not going to be able to solve the problem on the same level of the problem. This is where the Believer fits in. We come with answers. And those answers come through faith and innovation. "I wisdom dwell with prudence, **and find out knowledge** of witty inventions" (Prov. 8:12). Have you connected the dots yet? If I can ask for wisdom and God will liberally give it, and wisdom finds out the knowledge of witty inventions, then evidently prayer is for more than just talking to God.

When Believers innovate through faith, their success goes beyond personal or financial gain; it extends to fulfilling God's purposes on the earth. Innovative ideas that are birthed through God's wisdom often lead to products, services, or solutions that not only meet market needs but also address societal challenges, uplift communities, and bring glory to God. Innovation allows Believers to create businesses and organizations that reflect the Kingdom values of justice, compassion, service, and stewardship. When we apply faith and innovation together, our businesses become platforms for demonstrating the character of God in the marketplace. We serve as examples of how faith can drive progress and how God's wisdom can provide solutions to the most complex challenges.

Believers have an uncommon advantage in life and business. There is a reason why God plants us back into the world: **"And I say unto you, Make to yourselves friends of the mammon of unrighteousness; that, when ye fail, they may receive you into everlasting habitations" (Luke 16:9).** We have the All-Wise God on our side. We have to begin to see our spiritual practices as more than just communicating with God. But that they are also a means of downloading wisdom and knowledge that can keep us ahead of the curve and progressive in business. As a Believer, you can pray for wisdom and creative solutions. Make it a habit to seek God's wisdom daily. Pray specifically for innovative ideas, creative strategies, and new solutions that will set you apart in your industry.

> Innovation is a result of wisdom.

When God gives you an innovative idea or direction, step out in faith. Don't let fear or uncertainty hold you back. Trust that God will provide the resources, connections, and opportunities you need to bring that idea to life. Actively look for ways to improve processes, solve problems, and add value to your business or industry. Innovation requires a mindset of curiosity, creativity, and continuous improvement. Ask God to help you see things from a new perspective. You can work to cultivate a mind of innovation. As you innovate, ensure that your ideas align with the values of God's Kingdom. Seek to create products, services, or business practices that not only bring success but also make a positive impact on society and reflect God's character.

As Believers, we have access to a unique combination of faith and innovation that positions us for success in every area of life. The world of business shouldn't hate us. If a Believer is advancing a company or business and bringing into that organization the type of skillset, integrity, character, care, and innovation I am speaking of, even an Atheist would value their presence, because that Believer produces a fruit that's unquestionably and undeniably worthy of respect.

Proverbs 8:12 reminds us that wisdom leads to creative and innovative solutions—"witty inventions" that have the power to transform industries and communities. When we trust God for wisdom and step out in faith, we unlock divine innovation that sets us apart and allows us to impact the marketplace for the Kingdom of God. By combining faith and innovation, Believers can create businesses, products, and solutions that not only succeed but also demonstrate the power of God's wisdom in action. Success for the Believer is not just about financial gain but about advancing God's purposes on the earth, and faith-driven innovation is one of the most powerful tools to achieve that.

Chapter 4
Graced for Impact

For I say, through the grace given unto me, to every man that is among you, not to think of himself more highly than he ought to think; but to think soberly, according as God hath dealt to every man the measure of faith.

—**Romans 12:3**

The above passage speaks to the idea that each Believer has been given a "measure of faith" by God, and it's through this grace that they are equipped to fulfill their unique calling in both spiritual and earthly realms, including the marketplace. Faith is not uniform in size but measured out by God based on individual purpose and calling. It's an essential ingredient for achieving great things. This is why the text says that you can't think more highly than you ought. Faith combined with grace enables Christians to perform beyond their natural capacities. Grace is the divine enablement to accomplish what God has placed before us, and faith is the means by which we activate and walk in this grace. It is important to realize that no one is left out—every Christian has been given their portion of faith to fulfill their God-given assignment. Just as salvation is received by faith, so are our unique callings and assignments in the marketplace. When Christians understand that they are graced with the capacity to succeed, they can boldly step into arenas such as business, knowing that their measure of faith will sustain them (Eph. 2:8-9).

Nehemiah is an excellent example of someone who used his measure of faith to rebuild the walls of Jerusalem. Despite opposition and seemingly impossible odds, Nehemiah prayed and trusted God for favor. His faith not only provided protection but gave him the strategy to complete a massive project in just fifty-two days. Nehemiah's faith allowed him to accomplish what no one else could: **"The God of heaven will give us success. We his servants will start rebuilding" (Neh. 2:20)**. This faith-fueled leadership applies to the business world today as well.

I believe that there is an intersection where faith and business go together. **Faith isn't just for spiritual matters. It's critical for business, leadership, and decision-making.** When Christians operate from their measure of faith, they can tap into supernatural resources that enable them to make wise decisions, innovate, and persevere through challenges that others would not overcome. This grace doesn't just apply to the Christian entrepreneur, but to anyone in the marketplace. Faith requires action in the form of taking risks, pursuing innovation, and believing that God will provide where the natural might seem limited. Applying faith in business involves bringing your trust in God into the everyday decisions, challenges, and opportunities of the marketplace. Faith isn't just confined to religious practices; it's meant to be active in all areas of life, including your professional endeavors.

Here's how you can practically apply faith in business:

1. **Trust in God's provision and timing** – Faith requires trusting that God will provide what you need, when you need it, even when circumstances seem unfavorable, **"And my God will meet all your needs according to the riches of his glory in Christ Jesus" (Phil. 4:19).** In business, this means believing that God is your ultimate source of provision, not just profits or clients. Whether you are starting a new venture or navigating a challenging season, you must trust that God has a

plan and that His timing is perfect. God is faithful to provide for every need. Entrepreneurs and business leaders may face periods of uncertainty, whether it's financial constraints or a slow market. However, faith enables you to rest in the assurance that God will supply what's necessary for success, at the right time.

2. **Seeking divine wisdom for decision-making** - Faith is also about relying on God's wisdom instead of solely depending on human reasoning: "**Counsel is Mine, and sound wisdom: I am understanding; I have strength. By Me kings reign, and princes decree justice. By Me princes rule, and nobles, even all the judges of the earth" (Prov. 8:14-16).** In business, decision-making is critical, and faith requires you to trust that God's wisdom surpasses human understanding. This can be applied by consistently praying for guidance before making important business decisions, trusting God to lead you down the right path. By seeking God's wisdom through prayer and the Word, you invite Him into the decision-making process. Faith means trusting that God will give you insight and solutions that might not be obvious to others, **"but there is [a vital force] a spirit [of intelligence] in man, and the breath of the Almighty gives men understanding" (Job 32:8 AMPC).**

3. **Taking risks with confidence** - Faith often requires stepping out of your comfort zone and taking calculated risks. In business, faith in God can give you the boldness to pursue new ventures, expand your business, or innovate in areas where others are hesitant. Faith encourages you to move forward even when the outcome is uncertain because you believe that God is directing your steps. Applying faith means being willing to take steps that others might avoid because you have confidence that God is orchestrating something greater than what you can currently see. This could look like launching a product despite market uncertainties or investing in a vision that others doubt will succeed.

4. **Operating with integrity and trusting god for favor** - Faith in business also means operating with integrity, even when doing so could result in financial loss or missed opportunities: **"Then this Daniel was distinguished above the presidents and the satraps because an excellent spirit was in him, and the king thought to set him over the whole realm" (Dan. 6:3 AMPC).** Instead of compromising your values, faith allows you to trust that God will honor your commitment to righteousness and bless your business accordingly: **"Then the presidents and satraps sought to find occasion [to bring accusation] against Daniel concerning the kingdom, but they could find no occasion or fault, for he was faithful, nor was there any error or fault found in him" (v. 4).** Faith means trusting that God's way of doing business—operating with honesty, fairness, and integrity—will ultimately lead to success. When you resist cutting corners, remain truthful, and prioritize ethical practices, you position yourself to receive God's favor, which can open doors that human effort cannot.

5. **Faith to persevere through challenges** - Every business will face challenges, whether financial difficulties, competition, or internal struggles, **"and not only so, but we glory in tribulations also: knowing that tribulation worketh patience; and patience, experience; and experience, hope: and hope maketh not ashamed; because the love of God is shed abroad in our hearts by the Holy Ghost which is given unto us" (Rom. 5:3-4).** Faith doesn't mean you won't face hardship; it means you believe that God will help you overcome those challenges. Faith gives you the endurance to keep going when others give up. Applying faith in business means trusting that God is using even the tough times to refine you and your business. When challenges arise, instead of giving in to despair or fear, faith drives you to keep moving forward, knowing that God is working behind the scenes to bring about success.

6. **Sowing and reaping: giving in faith** - Another way to apply faith in business is through the principle of sowing and

reaping: **"Give, and it will be given to you. A good measure, pressed down, shaken together and running over, will be poured into your lap. For with the measure you use, it will be measured to you" (Luke 6:38 NIV).** As a business owner or leader, giving back, whether through tithing, charity, or reinvesting in people, requires faith. You trust that by giving, God will bless you with increase. **"Give generously, for your gifts will return to you later. Divide your gifts among many, for in the days ahead you yourself may need much help. Keep on sowing your seed, for you never know which will grow, perhaps it all will" (Ecc. 11:1-2,6 TLB).** Faith-driven businesses often experience growth and success because they operate from a mindset of abundance, not scarcity. By giving generously and trusting God to bring the return, you align your business with Kingdom principles.

7. **Surrounding yourself with faith-filled people** - **Proverbs 13:20** says, **"Walk with the wise and become wise, for a companion of fools suffers harm."** The people you surround yourself with in business can either help build your faith or drain it. Faith in business means being intentional about creating a network of like-minded individuals who also trust God and believe in His power to do the impossible. Surrounding yourself with other faith-filled leaders can strengthen your resolve and encourage you when you face obstacles: **"As iron sharpens iron, so a friend sharpens a friend" (Prov. 27:17).** Apply faith by seeking out partners, mentors, and employees who share your values and vision, trusting that God will bring the right people into your business. Faith-filled collaborations can lead to greater creativity, unity, and shared success: **"Plans succeed through good counsel; don't go to war without wise advice" (Prov. 20:18 NLT). "Plans go wrong for lack of advice; many advisers bring success" (Prov. 15:22 NLT).**

8. **Vision casting with God's perspective** - Having a God-given vision for your business requires faith to see beyond the

present circumstances: "And the Lord answered me, and said, **Write the vision, and make it plain upon tables, that he may run that readeth it. For the vision is yet for an appointed time, but at the end it shall speak, and not lie: though it tarry, wait for it; because it will surely come, it will not tarry (Hab. 2:2-3).** Faith means setting ambitious goals and dreaming big, believing that God can bring your vision to fruition, even if it seems impossible. When you align your business vision with God's purpose, you operate with a divine sense of direction and confidence: **"The wicked flee when no man pursueth: but the righteous are bold as a lion" (Prov. 28:1).** Faith helps you cast a vision that is rooted in God's plans for your business. It empowers you to keep working toward the goals God has given you, even when progress seems slow or obstacles arise.

Believers should always win. Victory is our portion, even in the marketplace. Applying faith in business means inviting God into every decision and trusting Him to guide, provide, and sustain your efforts. By relying on divine wisdom, taking bold risks, operating with integrity, and persevering through challenges, Christians can experience God's favor and success that goes beyond what they could achieve in their own strength. Faith transforms your approach to business, allowing you to move forward with confidence, knowing that God is with you every step of the way.

The Blessing—The Power to Get Wealth

Deuteronomy 8:18 declares, "But remember the Lord your God, for it is He who gives you the ability to produce wealth, and so confirms His covenant, which He swore to your ancestors, as it is today." This verse speaks directly to a powerful Kingdom principle: God has endowed His people with the divine ability to generate wealth. Wealth, in the Kingdom of God, is not merely financial prosperity; it is an extension of His covenant with His people, affirming His promise to bless, increase, and expand their influence on the earth. The marketplace is a significant avenue where God desires to release this power, equipping Believers with the resources and influence necessary to impact the world for His glory.

God's covenant with His people includes not just spiritual blessings but the ability to thrive and excel in every sphere of life—including business. This isn't just about personal success; it's about leveraging wealth and influence to advance God's purposes in the world. Kingdom wealth is a tool for transformation. When Christians access the divine power to generate wealth, they are partnering with God to bring about Kingdom solutions in society, create opportunities for others, and establish systems that honor God in the marketplace. Throughout scripture, we see examples of individuals who tapped into this Kingdom benefit and, as a result, did unimaginable things in their time.

> Believers can create brands that promote modesty and self-worth rather than materialism and exploitation.

Take Joseph, for example, who went from a slave in Egypt to second-in-command over the nation (Gen. 41:41-43). Joseph's wealth and influence were not the result of self-ambition but were born out of his faithfulness to follow God's wisdom. His ability to interpret Pharaoh's dream led to the creation of a strategic economic plan that not only saved Egypt but also positioned Joseph to control the distribution of resources during a time of famine. His success was a direct manifestation of the power God gave him to manage wealth and resources effectively. It should also be noted that Joseph never worked in the Church, though he was key to its survival. His gift of prophesying and interpreting dreams was for the governmental arena.

Another key figure is Solomon, a king whose wisdom and wealth were renowned throughout the world: **"Moreover, I will give you what you have not asked for, both wealth and honor, so that in your lifetime you will have no equal among kings" (I Kings 3:13).** Solomon's immense wealth was not just the result of his own hard work; it was a divine gift, a result of his obedience and submission to God's wisdom. Solomon understood that true wealth came from God, and he used it to build the temple, creating a legacy of worship that stood for generations.

Even in contemporary times, we see individuals like Truett Cathy, the founder of Chick-fil-A, and David Green, the founder of Hobby Lobby, who built business empires by following God's principles. Truett Cathy famously kept his restaurants closed on Sundays as a way to honor God, and despite the potential financial loss, his business thrived and became one of the most successful fast-food chains in the world. David Green started Hobby Lobby with a $600 loan, and through faithful stewardship, his business grew into a billion-dollar enterprise. These men understood that their success wasn't simply about their entrepreneurial skills, but about God's blessing on their businesses as they followed His principles.

For young entrepreneurs today, especially those equipped with business degrees and advanced knowledge of economic systems, it's essential to understand that the true key to success in the marketplace goes beyond strategies and market trends. It lies in activating the divine blessing and power to create wealth that God has already placed within His people.

When Believers operate in the marketplace with the power to get wealth, they have the opportunity to set a higher standard of ethics, integrity, and fairness. Believers can profoundly affect the marketplace through the power to get wealth by bringing Kingdom principles into business environments, industries, and economic systems. This power enables Believers to create wealth in ways that align with God's purposes, ultimately leading to transformation in the marketplace.

One of the most tangible ways Believers can impact the marketplace through wealth is by creating job opportunities and empowering others. Wealth creation allows Christian entrepreneurs to build businesses that provide employment, improve local economies, and offer fair wages and benefits. By using wealth to build businesses that serve others and provide meaningful work, Believers elevate the marketplace and the people within it: **"Seest thou a man**

diligent in his business? he shall stand before kings; he shall not stand before mean men" (Prov. 22:29).

The power to get wealth is not solely for personal enrichment, but also for advancing the Kingdom of God. Believers can affect the marketplace by using their financial resources to fund ministries, Churches, missionary work, and community projects that align with God's purposes.

Throughout history, individuals who have amassed great wealth have used their resources to support Kingdom initiatives. Take Billionaire Robert F. Smith. He and his family paid off the debts of his 2019 classmates that same year, a pledge gift that reached $34 million. He has dedicated much of his life to furthering educational opportunities for black and minority students. His personal gift of $50 million to help launch the Student Freedom Initiative was one of many that interconnect at the root of Smith's philanthropic mission to uplift black communities and provide the education and economic infrastructure to secure a solid future for generations of graduates to come.

Believers today can continue this legacy by strategically investing in Kingdom-building efforts. Whether it's supporting nonprofit organizations, building Christian schools, or providing resources to local communities, the wealth generated through Kingdom principles becomes a tool for the spread of the Gospel and societal transformation.

The power to get wealth also gives Believers the opportunity to influence entire industries and shift cultural narratives. When Believers rise to positions of wealth and influence, they gain a voice in shaping the direction of the industries they operate in. This influence can be used to promote righteousness, justice, and compassion within their field.

For example, a Believer who operates a media company can use their wealth and platform to create content that promotes wholesome, Godly values, influencing the entertainment industry for the better.

In the fashion industry, Believers can create brands that promote modesty and self-worth rather than materialism and exploitation. In government, Christian leaders with wealth can influence policies that reflect Kingdom values such as justice and care for the vulnerable. Believers who accumulate wealth are given a larger platform to be a light in their industry, influencing culture and systems from within. This ability to shape industry trends, media narratives, and societal standards is a direct result of wielding wealth as a tool for Kingdom influence:

> **Ye are the salt of the earth: but if the salt have lost his savour, wherewith shall it be salted? it is thenceforth good for nothing, but to be cast out, and to be trodden under foot of men. Ye are the light of the world. A city that is set on an hill cannot be hid. Neither do men light a candle, and put it under a bushel, but on a candlestick; and it giveth light unto all that are in the house. Let your light so shine before men, that they may see your good works, and glorify your Father which is in heaven (Matt. 5:13-16)**.

Another way Believers can affect the marketplace is by building generational wealth and leaving a legacy of faith-driven stewardship.

Generational wealth allows Believers not only to pass down financial assets but also to pass down values, wisdom, and influence. Wealth that is stewarded wisely can empower future generations to continue impacting the marketplace, advancing the Kingdom, and spreading the Gospel. It allows for long-term investments in businesses, properties, education, and charitable work that will continue to affect communities long after the original wealth was created. By building businesses or financial structures with a Kingdom perspective, Believers create opportunities for their descendants to walk in their calling and continue expanding God's Kingdom in their industries. This creates a ripple effect of influence that transcends one lifetime and ensures that the next generation is equipped with the resources and spiritual legacy to continue the work of transformation.

Finally, Believers who have been given the power to get wealth are positioned to provide innovative solutions to societal problems. Whether it's through funding technological advancements, creating affordable housing, or developing sustainable businesses, wealth gives Believers the capacity to address critical issues in society.

For instance, Christian entrepreneurs like Bill Bright, who co-founded Campus Crusade for Christ, utilized their wealth to create platforms for large-scale ministry that tackled both spiritual and social problems. Bright's vision extended beyond evangelism to include feeding the hungry, housing the homeless, and educating the next generation. His wealth allowed him to implement solutions that brought hope and change to millions.

In today's marketplace, Believers can leverage their wealth to address issues like poverty, inequality, education gaps, and environmental concerns. By doing so, they reflect the heart of God, who is concerned with justice and mercy: **"Is not this the kind of fasting I have chosen: to loose the chains of injustice and untie the cords of the yoke. . . . Is it not to share your food with the hungry and to provide the poor wanderer with shelter" (Isa. 58:6-7 NIV)?** Through wealth, Believers can answer this call, bringing tangible solutions to the world's deepest problems.

The Work of Your Hands

Nothing should remain the same or be returned in the same condition once touched or placed in the hands of a Believer: **"The Lord shall open unto thee his good treasure, the heaven to give the rain unto thy land in his season, and to <u>bless all the work of thine hand"</u> (Deut. 28:12).** God places a blessing on the work of your hands. When a Believer recognizes that their hands are anointed by God, everything they put their hands to, can manifest in its highest potential and at its greatest capacity. The key is not just diligent work, but understanding that divine favor is attached to your efforts. **"Do you see a man diligent and skillful in his**

business? He will stand before kings; he will not stand before obscure men" (Prov. 22:29).

There is a place where Kingdom businessmen should be found based on this scripture. When Believers in the marketplace are diligent and faithful in our work, we will gain influence and stand before great leaders, opening doors to new opportunities.

The first key to unlocking the anointing on your hands is **diligence**. Diligence in business involves consistent, focused effort in developing your skills, refining your products or services, and improving processes. It also means paying attention to details, staying disciplined in your work ethic, and taking ownership of every responsibility. As a Believer, your work ethic should reflect the excellence of God. Diligence means staying ahead of the curve by constantly seeking new ideas and innovations. Don't settle for mediocrity—push for innovation that solves real-world problems. Diligence, paired with faith, brings supernatural results. God anoints the work of your hands when you commit to working with excellence, consistently and faithfully.

God has given each of us unique talents and abilities that, when anointed, enable us to excel in our chosen fields. Proverbs 22:29 teaches that a person skilled and diligent in their work will not stand before obscure men, but before kings—this means that **skill and anointing will open doors of opportunity and influence**. Whether you're in leadership, management, design, marketing, or another field, your skill development is crucial. Commit to becoming a master of your craft. God's anointing flows where you are faithful to cultivate and refine the skills He has given you. When God anoints your hands, you have the capacity to bring innovative, effective solutions to complex problems. This positions your business to stand out in the marketplace.

Creativity in business is part of the anointing. Exodus 31:2-5 speaks of Bezalel, whom God filled with the Spirit of wisdom and creativity to craft beautiful works for the Tabernacle. Similarly, God anoints you with creativity to bring forth unique products, services, or solutions that reflect His glory and meet real needs. A business leader who recognizes that their hands are anointed will continually seek to grow in their skills and apply God-given creativity in ways that distinguish their work.

When the Bible says that a diligent person will "stand before kings," it's referring to influence and favor. As you operate with diligence and skill, God will position you before people of influence—whether they are leaders in your industry, business partners, or key decision-makers. This influence isn't just for personal gain, but for Kingdom impact. When your hands are anointed for work, everything you produce should reflect the excellence and integrity of God's Kingdom. Word will spread about the quality of your work, and this will attract high-level clients, partners, and opportunities. Standing before "kings" means that your work becomes a gateway to greater influence. Whether it's expanding into new markets, gaining larger contracts, or receiving investments, your diligence and excellence will open doors to greater opportunities. As you build your reputation through excellence, you can become a thought leader in your field. Whether through public speaking, publishing, or mentoring others, you can use your platform to influence others for the Kingdom of God. When your hands are anointed, you're not just working for personal success—you're being positioned to advance God's Kingdom through influence and leadership in the marketplace.

In the business world, the anointing of God's wisdom, skill, and favor on your hands can lead to remarkable success, setting you apart and positioning you for greater influence and impact. Throughout scripture, there is a recurring theme of God blessing the hands of His people. **Ps. 90:17 NIV** says, "May the favor of the Lord our God rest on us; establish the work of our hands for us—yes, establish the work of our hands." This blessing isn't just symbolic; it's a tangible promise that as Believers, we are empowered by God to succeed in what we set out to accomplish. The work of our hands is meant to flourish because it carries the touch of the divine. Not only that, but we are also representatives of the Kingdom of God.

This anointing can be seen in the life of Joseph. Although he faced many trials, from being sold into slavery to being falsely imprisoned, everything Joseph touched prospered. **Genesis 39:3** tells us that Joseph's master, Potiphar, "saw that the Lord was with him and that the Lord gave him success in everything he did." Even as a slave and later a prisoner, Joseph's hands were blessed by God. His diligence, combined with God's anointing, caused him to rise to power in Egypt, managing all the resources of the nation and saving countless lives during a famine. The blessing on his hands ensured that everything he managed was successful and fruitful.

The blessing of Deuteronomy 28:12 also comes with a responsibility: Believers are called to give their very best in all that they do, **"Whatever you do, work at it with all your heart, as working for the Lord, not for human masters" (Col. 3:23 NIV).** When Believers approach their work with a mindset of excellence, they are positioning themselves to experience the fullness of the blessing that God has placed on their hands. Excellence is not about perfection, but about doing everything with the understanding that God has anointed you for success. Daniel's hands were blessed by God, and he carried out his responsibilities with such excellence that he stood out among all his peers, **"Now Daniel so distinguished himself among the administrators and the satraps by his exceptional qualities that the king planned to set him over the whole kingdom" (Dan. 6:3 NIV).** His anointed hands positioned him to influence an entire empire and to be a vessel through which God revealed Himself to kings.

Faith is crucial to activating the anointing on their hands. The anointing on our hands requires us to step out in faith and believe that God will bless the work we do. This means approaching every project, business endeavor, or task with the expectation that God's favor will bring about supernatural results.

To fully embrace the anointing on your hands, it's important to take certain steps that position you to see the manifestation of God's blessing.

Here are several ways to activate this anointing in your life:

1. **Commit your work to the lord** - Before embarking on any project, make it a habit to commit it to God in prayer. Trust that as you submit your work to Him, He will guide and bless the outcome: **"Roll your works upon the Lord [commit and trust them wholly to Him; He will cause your thoughts to become agreeable to His will, and] so shall your plans be established and succeed" (Prov. 16:3 AMPC).**

2. **Pursue excellence** - Approach your work with a spirit of excellence, knowing that you are working for the Lord. **"Whatever your hand finds to do, do it with all your might" (Ecc. 9:10 NIV).** Whether it's a small task or a major project, always give your best because your anointed hands are capable of producing extraordinary results.

3. **Have faith in god's favor** - Believe that God's favor rests on your hands. Faith is the key that unlocks the supernatural. Step out confidently, knowing that God is with you and that His favor will cause your work to succeed. **"Whatever they do prospers" (Ps. 1:3).** When you trust in God's promise, you'll see divine results in your work.

4. **Keep a kingdom mindset** - Remember that the anointing on your hands is not just for personal success, but to advance God's Kingdom. Use your work and your wealth to serve others and glorify God. **"Seek first His kingdom and His righteousness, and all these things will be given to you as well" (Matt. 6:33 NIV).** As you keep a Kingdom focus, God will multiply the work of your hands for His glory.

5. **Be persistent and patient** - Sometimes the manifestation of God's blessing on your work may take time. Don't be discouraged if success isn't immediate: **"Let us not become weary in doing good, for at the proper time we will reap a harvest if we do not give up" (Gal. 6:9 NIV).** Keep pressing

forward, trusting that the anointing on your hands will produce fruit in due season.

There should be a notable and unquestionable difference when something is placed in the hands of a Believer or when a Believer touches something. Take Jacob for example. He worked for his father-in-law and increased his cattle mightily: **"And he said unto him, Thou knowest how I have served thee, and how thy cattle was with me. For it was little which thou hadst before I came, and it is now increased unto a multitude; and the Lord hath blessed thee since my coming: and now when shall I provide for mine own house also (Gen. 30:29-30)?** Jacob not only continued tending to his father-in-law's flock, but he set to simultaneously start his own business, and nothing went lacking in either one of their businesses. This story of Jacob also demonstrates how Believers should navigate between working for someone else while building their own and the ability to maintain a dual onus, order, and honesty to both. Nothing went lacking—everything went up because of the hands that were at work.

The anointing on a Believer's hands is a powerful revelation that transforms how we approach work. As Believers, when we recognize that our hands are blessed by God, we can step into any task, project, or business endeavor with confidence, knowing that success is inevitable. Through faith, excellence, and persistence, we can fully unlock the divine potential that God has placed in our hands, bringing about the highest manifestation of His will in the marketplace and beyond. Ultimately, the anointing of your hands to work is a divine partnership with God. It's not about striving in your own strength, but about yielding your abilities to God and allowing Him to work through you. Proverbs 16:3 says, **"Commit thy works unto the Lord, and thy thoughts shall be established."** As you dedicate your business and your hands to God, He establishes your plans and directs your path toward success.

Hidden Wisdom for the Marketplace

For the Kingdom entrepreneur, the Holy Spirit acts as a supernatural partner who can reveal things that are beyond human comprehension. In business, we often rely on research, data, and trends to make decisions. But **there is a higher level of insight available to those who are led by the Spirit**. As I Corinthians 2:10 says, "God hath revealed them unto us by His Spirit: for the Spirit searcheth all things, yea, the deep things of God." These "deep things" include not only spiritual truths but also practical wisdom for navigating the marketplace. Imagine the advantage you have when you are connected to the One who knows all things. Holy Spirit is not limited by time or human constraints; He sees the future, understands the complexities of every situation, and knows the heart of every individual you deal with in business. The Holy Spirit can give you insight into business transactions, partnerships, and opportunities that others may overlook. For example, when you're faced with a decision about entering a new market or forming a partnership, the Holy Spirit can reveal whether it will be fruitful or bring challenges. He can give you ideas for innovation that will set you apart from your competitors. He can alert you to things to come so you are not caught off guard. I like to say that the Holy Spirit makes you look smart.

> Through the Holy Spirit, you can access these "freely given" resources and apply them in your business.

While others are relying on their natural understanding, you can access supernatural wisdom that leads to success—a wisdom that is above human intellect. In addition to revealing hidden things, the Holy Spirit is also a guide who leads you step-by-step in your business journey. John 16:13 says, **"Howbeit when He, the Spirit of truth, is come, He will guide you into all truth: for He shall not speak of Himself; but whatsoever He shall hear, that shall He speak: and He will show you things to come."** As an entrepreneur, having the Holy Spirit as your guide means that you have access to the truth in every situation. He will guide you in your decision-making, helping you avoid pitfalls and make choices that align with

God's will. When you're in a boardroom, negotiating a deal, or planning your next move, the Holy Spirit can guide you in real time. He can give you discernment, helping you see beyond the surface level of a situation and understand the deeper implications. The Spirit may lead you to take a bold step that others don't understand, but because you trust His guidance, you can move forward with confidence. For example, you may be presented with a business opportunity that looks great on paper, but something in your spirit feels uneasy. That could be Holy Spirit guiding you to dig deeper or to pass on the opportunity altogether. Similarly, He may prompt you to pursue a project that seems risky but will ultimately bring great success. His guidance is not just for spiritual decisions but for every aspect of your business.

Often, entrepreneurs focus on strategy, marketing, and financials when it comes to closing business deals. While these elements are important, Kingdom entrepreneurs have an additional advantage: Holy Spirit can help you navigate business transactions in ways that others cannot. He gives you insight into the hearts of the people you are negotiating with, the future trajectory of markets, and the unseen risks and opportunities that come with each decision. I Corinthians 2:12 says, **"Now we have received, not the spirit of the world, but the spirit which is of God; that we might know the things that are freely given to us of God."** This means that there are resources, ideas, and strategies that God has already prepared for you. Through the Holy Spirit, you can access these "freely given" resources and apply them in your business. Whether it's closing a major deal or launching a new product, the Holy Spirit can give you the confidence and wisdom to navigate every step. Imagine negotiating a contract and being led by the Spirit to ask the right questions, raise concerns others may have missed, or structure the deal in a way that benefits both parties. This is not about manipulation, but about allowing the Holy Spirit to guide you toward agreements that are beneficial, ethical, and aligned with God's purposes.

As a Kingdom entrepreneur, cultivating a strong partnership with the Holy Spirit in your business is vitally important. Jesus told the disciples not to go without the Holy Spirit because there was a power that would come upon them after they received the Holy Spirit. I submit to you that this power is not just for godliness; this power is for the marketplace. Here are a few practical steps:

1. **Daily communion through prayer** – Just as you would consult with a business partner, regularly spend time in prayer, asking the Holy Spirit for guidance and insight. Before making decisions, seek His wisdom, and remain open to His leading. James 1:5 tells us that if we lack wisdom, we should ask God, who gives generously.

2. **Practice listening and obeying** – The Holy Spirit speaks in various ways, through the Word, in your spirit, and even through circumstances. Practice listening for His voice in your business meetings, in your planning sessions, and even in your day-to-day operations. Once you hear Him, be quick to obey, even if the direction seems unconventional.

3. **Ask for discernment** – In the marketplace, not every opportunity is from God, and not every deal is beneficial. Ask the Holy Spirit to give you discernment to recognize which opportunities align with God's will and which ones may lead to trouble. 1 John 4:1 tells us to "test the spirits" to see whether they are from God.

4. **Remain humble and dependent** – It's easy in the business world to become self-reliant, but a partnership with the Holy Spirit requires humility. Recognize that you need His wisdom and guidance, and be willing to rely on Him rather than your own understanding. **Proverbs 3:5-6** reminds us to trust in the Lord with all our heart and lean not on our own understanding.

As Kingdom-preneur, you have access to a supernatural advantage in the marketplace, and it's the Holy Spirit. He reveals things that no eye has seen and no ear has heard, giving you insight that goes beyond human understanding. He guides you into truth, helping you navigate every business decision with wisdom and discernment. By embracing the Holy Spirit as your partner in business, you are not only aligning your work with God's purposes but also positioning yourself for success that extends beyond the natural. Whether you're making critical business decisions, negotiating deals, or seeking the next innovative idea, the Holy Spirit is your source of supernatural wisdom and guidance, ready to lead you into all truth. Trust in Him, and let Him be your greatest business partner.

> **There is a revelation and an understanding that you desperately need to know about wisdom.** There is the wisdom of men and the wisdom of this world, and my language and my message were not set forth in **persuasive (enticing and plausible) words of wisdom**, but they were in demonstration of the [Holy] Spirit and power [a proof by the Spirit and power of God, operating on me and stirring in the minds of my hearers the most holy emotions and thus persuading them], So that your faith might not rest in the **wisdom of men** (human philosophy), but in the power of God. Yet when we are among the full-grown (spiritually mature Christians who are ripe in understanding), we do impart **a [higher] wisdom** (the knowledge of the divine plan previously hidden); but it is indeed not a wisdom of this present age or of this world nor of the leaders and rulers of this age, who are being brought to nothing and are doomed to pass away. . . . For this **world's wisdom** is foolishness (absurdity and stupidity) with God, for it is written, He lays hold of the wise in their [own] craftiness **(I Cor. 2:4-6, 3:19 AMPC)**.

The next is wisdom that is devilish, "Who is wise and understanding among you? Let them show it by their good life, by deeds done in the humility that comes from wisdom. But if you harbor bitter envy and selfish ambition in your hearts, do not boast about it or deny the truth. **Such 'wisdom'** does not come down from heaven but is **earthly, unspiritual, demonic**" (James 3:13-15 NIV).

The wisdom that Believers should be operating out of is the wisdom of God. And two of the most amazing things about the wisdom of God is that—number 1 she is crying out for you:

> **Wisdom cries aloud in the street, in the markets she raises her voice; at the head of the noisy streets she cries out; at the entrance of the city gates she speaks: "How long, O simple ones, will you love being simple? How long will scoffers delight in their scoffing and fools hate knowledge? If you turn at my reproof, behold, I will pour out my spirit to you; I will make my words known to you" (Prov. 1:20-23 ESV).**

Number 2, God wants to give it to you:

> **If any of you lacks wisdom, let him ask God, who gives generously to all without reproach, and it will be given him (James 1:5 ESV).**

I need for you to pay very close attention to what I'm about to share with you because, believe it or not, most of the successful Fortune 500 companies are operating by the wisdom of God. The sad irony is that most Believers are choosing man's wisdom and forfeiting the very wisdom that God wants to give to them because with Godly wisdom comes promotion, prosperity, prominence, pleasures, and protection. Did you just get what I just said—that **with Godly wisdom** comes (the added ingredients/what wisdom produces) is promotion, prosperity, prominence, pleasures, and protection:

> Blessed is the one who finds wisdom, and the one who gets understanding, **for the gain from her** is better than gain from silver and **her profit better than gold**. She is more precious than jewels, and **nothing you desire can compare with her**. **Long life is in her right hand; in her left hand are riches and honor**. **Her ways are ways of pleasantness**, and all **her paths are peace**. **She is a tree of life** to those who lay hold of her; those who hold her fast are called blessed. The Lord by wisdom founded the earth; by understanding He established the heavens;

> by His knowledge the deeps broke open, and the clouds drop down the dew. **My son, do not lose sight of these—keep sound wisdom and discretion,** and **they will be life for your soul and adornment for your neck. Then you will walk on your way securely, and your foot will not stumble (Prov. 3:13-23 ESV).**

Think of all the Believers who are in business and are functioning only from what a certificate or degree gave them, or from what they learned—even those who are guessing, when they have available to them an untapped well of wisdom from God that will cause them to excel in the business sector.

Failure should not be the Believer's quota, not when the Believer can ask God for wisdom, and He will give it liberally. There should not be any question as to who the promotion, raise, or award is going to if a Believer is involved or in the company. What we have done as the Church, to some degree, is put persecution in the wrong place. Persecution happens because of the fruit a Believer produces. No one persecutes a Christian who produces no fruit, because without fruit, no one knows they are a Christian. Jesus and the disciples were being persecuted *because of* the fruit they produced. In the same way, believers should be experiencing persecution for always being the ones who are acknowledged. But this is also what God uses as a witness and hook to the world. This is what opens the heart of the unsaved with the question of, "What you are doing that's causing you to outclass, outpace, and outproduce everyone else?" This is what the Bible meant by letting your light shine before men (Matt. 5:16).

Just like we were told not to go into the world and be a witness without the power of Holy Spirit, because the power is needed to produce the results, we should not go into the marketplace with ministry without the wisdom of God, because it's the wisdom that produces Kingdom results:

> **I wisdom dwell with prudence, and find out knowledge of witty inventions. Riches and honour are with me; yea, durable riches and righteousness. My fruit is better than gold, yea, than fine gold; and my revenue than choice silver.**

> **I lead in the way of righteousness, in the midst of the paths of judgment: that I may cause those that love me to inherit substance; and I will fill their treasures.... For whoso findeth me findeth life, and shall obtain favour of the Lord (Prov. 8:12,18-21,35).**

King Solomon was noted as the richest man alive. Not only that, but he was a very affluent businessman. It was wisdom that made Solomon rich. It wasn't mere intellect, nor just the fact that he was king. When God asked Solomon what he wanted, he could have asked for riches or anything, but even in his asking, Solomon was wise. Solomon asked for wisdom. I used to wonder why he asked for wisdom. Then when I started reading Proverbs, I found out why. The first reason is because he realized that he needed wisdom in order to lead effectively—and not just any wisdom, but God's. Secondly wisdom is the principle thing—it's the first thing, the door to all the rest. But this third reason is astounding. I know you want to make it big. You want your business and brand to be world known. You have big dreams and big aspirations. All of that is good. But the wisdom of God is the key. I don't know how Solomon knew this. I would assume that Solomon just wanted to please God, make His name known, and lead his people the right way. What Solomon may or may not have known is that to ask for wisdom is to ask for riches: **"Riches and honour are with me; yea, durable riches and righteousness" (Prov. 8:18)**.

The story of Jacob's supernatural wisdom in increasing his cattle provides a powerful example of how God can grant unique strategies and insights to solve business challenges and create unprecedented success in the marketplace. Jacob's story, found in Genesis 30:37-43, illustrates how God's wisdom goes beyond human understanding, empowering Believers to come up with innovative solutions that defy conventional thinking. For the Kingdom entrepreneur, this story is a reminder that God is not limited by natural circumstances and that, through prayer and faith, Believers can access divine wisdom to achieve supernatural outcomes.

Jacob had worked for his father-in-law, Laban, for many years, and despite his hard work, Laban repeatedly changed his wages and treated him unfairly. But God had a plan to bless Jacob, even in the midst of an unjust situation. After years of service, Jacob negotiated an agreement with Laban where he would take all the speckled and spotted sheep and goats as his wages. However, these types of animals were rare in Laban's flock. It seemed like a poor deal for Jacob from a human perspective, but God gave him supernatural wisdom to turn the situation in his favor.

Jacob used an unconventional method that seemed strange by natural standards. He took sticks of poplar, almond, and plane trees, peeled white strips on them, and placed them in front of the watering troughs where the animals mated. As a result, the flocks began to produce offspring that were speckled, streaked, and spotted—precisely the kind of animals Jacob had claimed as his wages. This led to a significant increase in his flocks, making him wealthy and prosperous.

Jacob's strategy was not just a clever trick—it was divine wisdom given by God. In Genesis 31:10-12, Jacob explains that God revealed this strategy to him in a dream. What seemed like an impossible situation was turned around through God's intervention, showing that His wisdom can bring about results that far exceed natural expectations.

For today's Kingdom entrepreneur, this story is a powerful example of how seeking God's wisdom can lead to innovative and unthinkable solutions in business. Just as God gave Jacob insight into how to increase his flocks, He can provide you with supernatural strategies that go beyond conventional business practices.

Just as Jacob received divine wisdom through a dream, the Believer has access to God's supernatural insight. James 1:5 encourages us to ask God for wisdom, saying, **"If any of you lack wisdom, let him ask of God, that giveth to all men liberally, and upbraideth not; and it shall be given him."** In the marketplace, there are often situations that seem impossible or challenges that appear insurmountable. However, when you seek God's wisdom in prayer, He can reveal solutions that no one else could have thought of. In business, this might mean the following:

- Asking God for insight on how to develop a new product or service that fills a gap in the market.
- Praying for wisdom on how to negotiate deals that seem unfavorable but could turn into major opportunities.
- Seeking divine strategies on how to position your business differently from competitors.

God's wisdom is not bound by industry standards or market trends. He can give you insight that transcends the normal way of doing things, leading to success that others might not even consider possible.

Jacob's strategy of using peeled sticks in front of the flocks was unconventional and defied natural logic. Yet it worked because it was rooted in divine wisdom. Similarly, God often gives Believers ideas that are outside the norm—innovations that disrupt industries, solve complex problems, or lead to new ways of doing business.

The marketplace is constantly changing, and the most successful entrepreneurs are those who innovate. However, innovation for the Believer isn't just about creativity or thinking outside the box—it's about tapping into God's limitless wisdom. What others may see as a limitation, God can turn into an opportunity through a unique strategy.

For example, during economic downturns or times of crisis, God may give you an unconventional strategy to pivot your business or launch a new initiative that others may not see. Just as Jacob's strategy increased his wealth despite the odds, God's wisdom can lead you to success in times when the market is uncertain or unfavorable.

Jacob's story reminds us that God is not limited by natural circumstances. Even when Laban changed Jacob's wages multiple times in an attempt to cheat him, God ensured that Jacob would prosper. This is a powerful reminder that, as a believer, your success is not dependent solely on market conditions or what seems possible in the natural. When God is your source, He can bring supernatural results that defy human logic. Ephesians 3:20 says that God is able to do **"exceeding abundantly above all that we ask or think, according to the power that worketh in us."** In business, this means that God can take what seems like a disadvantage or a dead-end situation and turn it into a path for growth and success. Just as Jacob's strategy led to an explosion of wealth, God can bring unexpected results when you follow His guidance. In your business, this might look like a breakthrough idea that leads to exponential growth, finding favor in negotiations or contracts that others may overlook, or receiving divine insight into timing—knowing exactly when to invest, launch, or expand.

It's important to note that **Jacob acted on the wisdom God gave him**. He didn't just receive the vision and wait passively—he took bold steps to implement what God had shown him. For Kingdom entrepreneurs, it's essential to act on the wisdom God provides. When God gives you a strategy, it may seem unconventional or even risky, but by stepping out in faith, you position yourself to experience the supernatural results that come with obedience.

Business often involves risk, but when that risk is guided by divine wisdom, it leads to reward. Jacob's boldness in following God's instructions serves as an example of how faith and action go hand-in-hand in the marketplace. When you trust in God's ability to bring supernatural results, you are not limited by what you see in the natural. Just as Jacob trusted in the vision God gave him, you can trust that when God gives you wisdom, He will bring about the results, even if they seem impossible at first.

As a Kingdom entrepreneur, you have access to supernatural wisdom that can lead to breakthrough success. In a world where business decisions are often driven by data and conventional practices, the Believer has an advantage—God's wisdom. Just as Jacob received an unconventional strategy that multiplied his wealth, you, too, can ask God for wisdom to innovate, solve problems, and come up with solutions that others might never consider.

God's wisdom is not just for spiritual matters but for every aspect of life, including business. When you seek His guidance, trust His process, and act boldly on the wisdom He provides, you can experience supernatural results that go beyond human understanding. Like Jacob, you can prosper in the marketplace, even when the odds are against you, because God's wisdom will lead you to unthinkable resolve and success.

Are you operating from the wisdom of God? Read the book, get educated, get the degree, ascribe for higher learning—all of that is good and notable. But ask God to give you His wisdom, **"for by me [Wisdom from God] your days shall be multiplied, and the years of your life shall be increased" (Prov. 9:11 AMPC).** If you want a real sustainable promotion that you do not have to fight to obtain or attain, you need the wisdom of God: "**Get wisdom**, get understanding: forget it not; neither decline from the words of my mouth. Forsake her not, and **she shall preserve thee**: love her, and **she shall keep thee. Wisdom is the principal thing**; therefore get wisdom: and with all thy getting get understanding. Exalt her, and **she shall promote thee: she shall bring thee to honour**, when thou dost embrace her. **She shall give to thine head an ornament of grace: a crown of glory shall she deliver to thee" (Prov. 4:5-9)**.

Chapter 5

Intrapreneurship

His master said to him, Well done, you upright (honorable, admirable) and faithful servant! You have been faithful and trustworthy over a little; I will put you in charge of much. Enter into and share the joy (the delight, the blessedness) which your master enjoys.
—Matthew 25:23 AMPC

You do not have to be the boss to be the boss. Many have been misled. Everyone isn't called to head their own thing. Jesus emptied Himself of Sovereignty and was formed into the likeness of man. This means that the earthly ministry of Jesus was an example of running a Kingdom on the behalf of the owner: **"Do you not believe that I am in the Father and the Father is in Me? The words that I say to you I do not speak on My own authority, but <u>the Father who dwells in Me does His works</u> (John 14:10 ESV)**.

Leadership within someone else's business, commonly referred to as intrapreneurship, allows for substantial influence. An intrapreneur is someone who acts with an entrepreneurial mindset while working within an established organization. They are empowered to innovate, lead teams, and drive change, even though they may not have a financial stake in the company. Kingdom entrepreneurs can thrive in such roles by applying the Godly principles of stewardship and leadership, gaining influence and headship over critical areas of the business. In the business world, this translates into the idea that leadership is not confined to ownership but is rooted in your ability to solve problems, manage teams effectively, and drive value within an organization. If you can faithfully lead and steward resources within someone else's company, you can still experience significant influence and success.

In the marketplace, both entrepreneurship and intrapreneurship are valuable pathways to success, each with its own unique demands and opportunities. While entrepreneurs create and lead their own ventures, intrapreneurs operate within someone else's organization, often leading major initiatives, innovating from within, and driving the business toward greater success. Both roles require vision, leadership, and creativity, but they manifest in different contexts.

> You do not have to be the boss *to be the boss.*

Joseph's life presents a powerful biblical example of intrapreneurship is the story of Joseph, who served as a leader under both Potiphar and Pharaoh: **"Joseph found favor in his eyes and became his attendant. <u>Potiphar put him in charge of his household</u>, and <u>he entrusted to his care everything he owned</u>" (Gen. 39:4).** His story is a template for how Believers can thrive in positions where they are managing or leading in someone else's business or organization while remaining faithful to God and achieving remarkable success. Even though Joseph was serving in Potiphar's house as a slave, he was given the opportunity to act as an intrapreneur, running Potiphar's entire household and making decisions that would lead to its prosperity. Similarly, after his unjust imprisonment and eventual rise to power in Egypt, **Joseph was put in charge of Pharaoh's entire kingdom, "So Pharaoh said to Joseph, 'I hereby put you in charge of the whole land of Egypt'" (Gen. 41:41).** Joseph's ability to manage others' resources with excellence is a prime example of intrapreneurship. He didn't own the assets he managed, but his wisdom, leadership, and stewardship brought great success and prosperity to those he served. Joseph's story shows that you don't have to own the business to have a profound impact on it.

Intrapreneurs can thrive and become highly successful within an existing structure, using their skills and leadership to innovate, improve processes, and create value for the organization. They don't take on the risks of ownership, but they often have the freedom to lead and influence the direction of the company. Had it not been a directive from God for me to open a business, I would have been fine operating in another person's business. I have seen many people who were once successful fail at being entrepreneurs because they felt the need to move out on their own, when in fact their gift and talent worked best while under another. This is an easy vice to fall victim to because intrapreneurs often have the mindset of an entrepreneur but work best within the safety and resources of a larger organization.

In today's business world, we can see this reflected in people like Sheryl Sandberg, the COO of Facebook. She is not the founder of the company, but her leadership within the organization has been instrumental in its growth. Sandberg's role as an intrapreneur allows her to innovate, drive change, and make strategic decisions that impact the company's success, all while working within the framework established by the original founder, Mark Zuckerberg.

Another example is Tim Cook, who took over the operational leadership of Apple under Steve Jobs. While Jobs was the visionary entrepreneur behind Apple, Cook was the intrapreneur who made sure that the company ran smoothly and efficiently. His operational expertise helped Apple grow into the world's largest company by market capitalization. After Jobs' passing, Cook transitioned into the role of CEO, but much of his success was built on the foundation of leading from within as an intrapreneur.

While entrepreneurship and intrapreneurship are different, both roles require a commitment to excellence, innovation, and leadership. Whether you're leading your own company or someone else's, the principles of stewardship apply equally. **"Whatever you**

do, work at it with all your heart, as working for the Lord, not for human masters" (Col. 3:23 NIV). This scripture is a guiding principle for both entrepreneurs and intrapreneurs alike. Whether you own the business or are leading within it, your work is ultimately for God's glory.

The story of Joseph shows that success isn't just about ownership; it's about faithful stewardship of what God has entrusted to you. Joseph didn't need to own Pharaoh's kingdom to lead with excellence and make a significant impact. Similarly, many of today's intrapreneurs work within someone else's organization but lead with the same vision, creativity, and leadership that entrepreneurs use to build their own companies.

Intrapreneurship is a valid and valuable path to leadership and success in the marketplace. Although intrapreneurs innovate from within existing structures, they are not limited to seeing opportunities and capitalizing on them for success. There are a plethora of intrapreneurs who have achieved their life dreams and even reached multi-millionaire status. Just because their names are not on the signage and they don't sign the checks does not mean that they don't sign a check.

You can thrive in headship without owning the company. Many Kingdom entrepreneurs assume that true leadership in the marketplace is tied to ownership—owning a company, making the final decisions, and having the authority that comes with being the boss. However, this perspective overlooks the fact that leadership can thrive and be exercised powerfully even within someone else's company.

The Bible offers a profound principle for those leading within businesses they don't own. In Luke 16:12, Jesus teaches, **"And if ye have not been faithful in that which is another man's, who shall give you that which is your own?"** This scripture emphasizes an important truth for Kingdom entrepreneurs: leadership and headship don't always require ownership. Faithful leadership in managing someone else's resources, vision, and enterprise can position you for influence and even greater opportunities. In today's corporate landscape, many talented individuals find themselves leading divisions, managing key projects, or spearheading initiatives in companies they do not own. Their leadership influence, however, remains profound because of their ability to steward their responsibilities with excellence. Luke 16:12 highlights the importance of stewardship. As a leader within someone else's business, your ability to be a faithful steward of what has been entrusted to you is critical. Stewardship is about managing resources, people, and processes in a way that honors the owner's vision while maximizing the potential of the business.

In business terms, stewardship involves understanding the financial goals of the company, aligning your team's efforts with the company's strategy, and being proactive in problem-solving. Whether you are leading a department, overseeing a product launch, or managing a critical project, the way you handle these responsibilities showcases your leadership skills and builds trust with the organization's owners and stakeholders. When a business owner sees you faithfully stewarding their company's resources, whether it's time, people, or finances, they are more likely to entrust you with greater responsibility. This is where headship comes in. By consistently delivering results, managing effectively, and aligning your leadership with the overall vision of the company, you can gain significant authority within the business, even if you don't hold an ownership stake.

So, how does a Kingdom entrepreneur exercise headship within someone else's company? It begins with key leadership skills that are valued in any business setting:

1. **Vision alignment and execution** - Great leaders understand the importance of aligning with the overarching vision of the company. Even if you are not the owner, you can still contribute to shaping the future of the business by executing projects and strategies that support the company's vision. When you take ownership of initiatives and deliver exceptional results, you position yourself as a trusted leader. This is critical in corporate

leadership. Successful leaders don't just manage the status quo; they innovate, improve processes, and create value. For instance, if you're in charge of a division, you might take the initiative to improve operational efficiency, increase customer satisfaction, or develop new products that boost revenue. In doing so, you show your capacity to lead with vision and take the company to the next level.

2. **Strategic decision-making** – Another key leadership skill that enables headship is the ability to make strategic decisions. Whether it's navigating a crisis, managing change, or identifying growth opportunities, the ability to think strategically sets you apart as a leader. Strategic decision-making is highly valued by business owners because it shows that you are thinking about the long-term success of the company, not just your immediate responsibilities.

   Leaders in non-ownership roles can influence company direction by presenting innovative solutions, analyzing market trends, and developing strategies that align with the business's goals. Your ability to think strategically and guide your team through complex decisions will establish your headship within the organization.

3. **Developing and leading teams** – Great leaders build and lead strong teams. Even in someone else's business, the way you lead and develop people under your charge demonstrates your leadership capacity. Investing in your team's growth, providing mentorship, and fostering a collaborative work environment can significantly elevate your leadership status in the company. As you develop strong teams that deliver high performance, the company's leadership will increasingly rely on you for key projects and decisions. Your influence expands beyond your immediate role, and you become a vital part of the organization's success.

4. **Innovating within the organization** – Innovation is often associated with entrepreneurship, but it is just as critical within

established businesses. Intrapreneurs who innovate from within, whether through new products, services, processes, or business models, are highly valued in any company. If you can bring fresh ideas and improvements that increase the company's competitive advantage, you will be seen as a leader regardless of ownership. Bringing creative solutions to market challenges and seizing new opportunities demonstrates your ability to think entrepreneurially within an organization. Innovation showcases your capacity for leadership and positions you for greater influence.

5. **Building trust and credibility** - Trust is a fundamental component of leadership. As you lead in someone else's business, building trust with both the ownership and your team is essential. Trust comes from consistently delivering results, operating with integrity, and making decisions that are in the best interest of the company. When owners see that they can trust you with critical responsibilities and decisions, you gain headship and influence, even without owning the business. Your credibility within the organization grows, and you become a key player in its success.

Faithfulness in leading within someone else's company often opens the door to greater opportunities, both within that business and beyond. Luke 16:12 teaches us that when we are faithful in managing someone else's resources, God opens doors for us to step into greater ownership and responsibility. Your success in leading within an organization can lead to new opportunities for partnership, equity stakes, or even the opportunity to start your own business.

In the marketplace, many executives and leaders begin their careers managing parts of larger companies, only to later move into ownership roles or create their own ventures. By exercising faithful leadership in your current role, you position yourself for future growth and opportunities. Just as Joseph was elevated from managing a household to ruling over Egypt, your ability to steward leadership well within someone else's organization can propel you to even greater influence and success in the marketplace.

Kingdom entrepreneurs need to understand that leadership is not limited to those who own businesses. Faithful stewardship in leadership, even within someone else's company, is a pathway to influence and headship. By demonstrating leadership through vision alignment, strategic decision-making, team development, innovation, and building trust, you can thrive in roles where you have significant responsibility and impact without being the owner. In the business world, leadership is about how you manage, lead, and add value. Your headship is not determined by whether or not you hold the title of owner; it is determined by your ability to lead effectively, create results, and steward the resources entrusted to you. When you do this faithfully, you set yourself up for both present success and future opportunities.

It Fits Your Faith

> The people who do great in life are those who are resolute in who they are and how they do it.

Most Believers have heard the story of David and Goliath and how David killed Goliath with a sling and a stone. But there is an amazing takeaway from part of the story that I want to bring to your attention as a businessperson who seeks to achieve major things. The first part is Saul's testimony of David: **"And Saul said to David, Thou art not able to go against this Philistine to fight with him: for thou art but a youth, and he a man of war from his youth" (I Sam. 17:33).** David is first discredited and considered incapable. Saul then seeks to help David accomplish what he first thought to be impossible victory and arms David with his armor:

> **And Saul armed David with his armour, and he put an helmet of brass upon his head; also he armed him with a coat of mail. 39 And David girded his sword upon his armour, and he assayed to go; for he had not proved it. And David said unto**

> **Saul, I cannot go with these; for I have not proved them. And David put them off him (I Sam. 17:38-39).**

The problem is that it does not fit David, not in the sense of him not being able to wear it, but because it **does not fit with his ability.** David was a shepherd who lived out in the field with the sheep. Shepherds did not wear armor like soldiers, and what they used to fight and defend fit the sheep was much different. In the eyes of Saul, David could not use a sling to kill a giant. But what was simply a sling to Saul was a weapon to David because he knew how to use it. However, Saul didn't need to see it; David only needed to know it. And here lies the part of the story that I wanted you to see: **that David was bold and confident enough to take off what didn't fit and go with what did.** Like David, you have been fitted with a faith that has goliath potential. David had all he needed. He just had to make the decision to go with what fit him, "**and he took his staff in his hand, and chose him five smooth stones out of the brook, and put them in a shepherd's bag which he had, even in a scrip; and his sling was in his hand: and he drew near to the Philistine" (I Sam. 17:40)**. Now, he was ready! He was himself—who God made him to be and how God created him to do it. Saul's way would have been defeat, but David's fit gave him the giant's head. Here's the moral of the story—the size of a thing has no relevance to whether or not you will see victory, as long as your approach is in the way that fits your faith. **So <u>David prevailed</u> over the Philistine <u>with a sling and with a stone</u>, and smote the Philistine, and slew him; but there was no sword in the hand of David (I Sam. 17:50).** What may not be much in the life of someone else is the very measure of faith given to you for victory. People who do great in life are those who are resolute in who they are and how they do it—those who aren't trying to fit a mold they weren't made from.

Every Believer is given a measure of faith. The word *measure* refers to one's degree of, amount, or unique level and special ability to perform. It also means what you have been fitted to do versus someone else. Daniel, Hananiah, Mishael, and Azariah had abilities and skills that others did not have. They were **"children in whom**

was no blemish, but well favoured, and skillful in all wisdom, and cunning in knowledge, and understanding science, and such as had ability in them to stand in the king's palace, and whom they might teach the learning and the tongue of the Chaldeans" (Dan. 1:4). All of the children of Israel did not have the fit that the king was looking for. The scripture said that the king said to find **"certain"** children (Daniel 1:3). This doesn't mean that God is a respecter of person; it just means that He doesn't give us all the same fit. You are fit for something—you just have to discover yours.

I am a teacher, and I'm dramatic at times. *Theatrical* is a better word. I move a lot and am somewhat quirky. I tried to stop and be more astute. After two services, I realized that I wasn't being who I was. I was attempting to fit a mold that I wasn't made from. It felt stiff, no fluidity. The message seemed to be losing its simplicity. I realized that I was outside of the fit of my faith. I immediately shifted, and I could even feel that the Holy Spirit was pleased with me being who I was so that He could be who He was through me. **You never give up who you are, because you lose how God made you.** You are not made for everything, but the thing(s) you are made for, they fit your faith. You have special abilities that are perfectly tailored to their specific makeup, purpose, and even flow: **"For by the grace given me I say to every one of you: Do not think of yourself more highly than you ought, but rather think of yourself with sober judgment, in accordance with the faith God has distributed to each of you" (Rom. 12:3 NIV).** This scripture elucidates that faith is apportioned by God to every individual. The measure of faith given to each person is enough to fulfill the calling and tasks set before them. The thing that causes most Believers to miss their mark is them focusing on what's working for others and trying to mimic that, rather than discovering their own distinctiveness and aptitude that lies within and building on that.

God gives every person three things: spiritual gifts, natural talents, and acquired skills. And every man doesn't operate or function the same. Your grace may not be identical to that of others, but it is no less valuable. Don't fall into the trap of comparison, thinking that because you're not an entrepreneur, your abilities are somehow secondary. Instead, lean into the unique gifts and abilities God has given you. Your role as an intrapreneur is vital because you have been fitted for this moment, this assignment, and this opportunity. When you trust that what God has deposited in you is enough, you can step into any challenge with confidence. You aren't there to compete; you are there to DO BUSINESS.

The marketplace needs what you have, and your contribution has the potential to shape the future of your organization and bring glory to the Kingdom of God. It's our own fit of faith that makes the difference: **"Having then gifts differing according to the grace that is given to us" (Rom. 12:6a).** John wanted to stop some men from healing only because they weren't doing it the way Jesus and His disciples did. But Jesus stopped John, and John spoke up, **"'Teacher, we saw a man using your Name to expel demons and we stopped him because he wasn't in our group.' Jesus wasn't pleased. 'Don't stop him. No one can use My Name to do something good and powerful, and in the next breath slam Me. If he's not an enemy, he's an ally'" (Mark 9:38-40 MSG).** I know you aren't casting out demons, so you may think this story isn't relative. However, I shared this to ask you, what you are casting away from you because it doesn't seem to fit the crowd or what everyone else is doing? Have you seen your fit as being a curse or a blessing in disguise? If you look like everyone else, what makes you different or sets you apart?

Faith is more than just a belief in God. It's a degree of operation that God gives every man, **"according as God hath dealt to every man the measure of faith" (Rom. 12:3d)**. This is where your greatness lies. If you can discover your fit, the possibilities are endless. The marketplace doesn't need another replica; it needs a bold original: **"Now to Him who is able to do immeasurably more than all we ask or imagine, according to His power that is at work within us" (Eph. 3:20 NIV)**. There is a divine power at work within you that can do far more than you can even imagine. This scripture is a reminder that God has equipped you with more than enough to get the job done. The dreams, ideas, and solutions He's placed within you have the potential to transform your organization and even industries.

You have an abundance of potential. When you approach your role from a place of faith in God's provision and in your own abilities, you can go beyond the ordinary and operate in the extraordinary. Your role as an intrapreneur is not just about doing your job; it's about creating value, leading with vision, and exceeding the expectations of those around you. God has not called you to operate in fear but in boldness, **"For God gave us a spirit not of fear but of power and love and self-control" (II Tim. 1:7 ESV).** Boldness is key in exceeding expectations as an intrapreneur. When you recognize that God is your source and that you are fitted with divine ability, it becomes easier to take calculated risks, innovate, and offer solutions that others may not see.

Your boldness is what will separate you from the average employee. While others may simply do their job, you are called to go above and beyond. Boldly offer new ideas, confidently present your strategies, and be unafraid to lead when the opportunity presents itself. The marketplace rewards those who are willing to take courageous action. You can be the catalyst for change and the driver of success, not just for the company but also for yourself.

Purpose Driven

Many pursue success driven by profits, expansion, and market dominance. However, for the Kingdom-minded entrepreneur or professional, success is defined by a deeper calling—a purpose-driven business that aligns with God's mission and values. A purpose-driven business is one that integrates the leader's faith and values into the core of the business model, ensuring that the pursuit of success is not just about profit but about advancing God's Kingdom through ethical practices, serving others,

> A purpose-driven business is not just about making a living; it's about fulfilling a calling.

and stewarding resources wisely. A purpose-driven business is a business that operates with a clear sense of mission and values that go beyond making money. Its mission is often rooted in serving others, addressing societal challenges, and making a positive impact on the world, all while reflecting the principles of the Kingdom of God. **Proverbs 16:3** says, **"Commit thy works unto the Lord, and thy thoughts shall be established."** The Amplified Classic Edition says it like this: **"Roll your works upon the Lord [commit and trust them wholly to Him; He will cause your thoughts to become agreeable to His will, and] so shall your plans be established and succeed."** This scripture reminds us that when we align our work with God's purposes, He will guide our plans and establish our success. A purpose-driven business seeks to honor God in every aspect—how it treats employees, engages with customers, and contributes to the community. It's a business that views success not just in terms of financial profit but also in terms of the positive impact it makes in the lives of others and in advancing the Kingdom.

When a business has a clear sense of purpose, it gives clarity to decision-making, strategy, and operations. Purpose acts as a guiding light that helps the business stay focused on what truly matters, even in times of uncertainty or challenge. With purpose, leaders can align their goals with long-term impact rather than short-term gains. A purpose-driven business leader understands that success is not about chasing every opportunity but about staying true to the mission that God has called them to. This helps leaders avoid distractions and stay focused on fulfilling their God-given mandate: **"Let your eyes look right on [with fixed purpose], and let your gaze be straight before you. Consider well the path of your feet, and let all your ways be established and ordered aright (Prov. 4:25-26 AMPC)**. Vision and purpose are closely connected, and without a clear sense of purpose, businesses can lose direction and ultimately fail to reach their potential.

Purpose attracts loyalty. Customers, employees, and partners are drawn to businesses that stand for something greater than profit. A clear purpose creates a sense of loyalty and trust because it reflects authenticity and integrity. Forbes reports that in the entrepreneurial world, a sense of purpose often stands out as an essential attribute to success. The World Economic Forum (WEF) suggests that businesses with a strong sense of purpose inspire trust, and those with solid and effective purpose strategies often see great returns. Most business leaders (82 percent) say that the primary focus of their company's purpose strategy is to create business value. The report went on to say that many higher schools are adding purpose-driven entrepreneurship course to meet current market conditions.

When customers see that a business is committed to positive values such as fairness, justice, and service, they are more likely to support it. Employees also benefit from working in a purpose-driven business. People want to work for companies that give them meaning and the opportunity to contribute to something bigger than themselves. A purpose-driven business empowers employees to see how their daily work contributes to a larger mission, creating a sense of fulfillment and motivation.

Purpose also leads to longevity. Businesses that are purpose-driven tend to have a longer lifespan because their focus is on building sustainable success, rather than just immediate profit: **"Be not wise in thine own eyes: fear the Lord, and depart from evil. It shall be health to thy navel, and marrow to thy bones (Prov. 4:7-8).** When a business prioritizes Kingdom values and purpose, God provides the resources and opportunities necessary for long-term success.

Purpose-driven businesses are also more resilient in difficult times because they are built on a foundation of faith, integrity, and mission. While market trends and economic conditions may fluctuate, a purpose-driven business remains steadfast in its values, which provides stability and continuity. When businesses operate with purpose, they have the potential to bring about lasting change. Purpose-driven businesses transform industries, influence cultures, and solve real-world problems in ways that glorify God.

As a Christian business leader, you have the opportunity to model Kingdom values in the marketplace, showing the world that businesses can succeed while serving others, operating with integrity, and fulfilling a higher mission. A purpose-driven business is not just about making a living; it's about fulfilling a calling. It's about using the platform of business to honor God, serve others, and create meaningful impact. When we align our businesses with God's Kingdom purposes, we position ourselves for both spiritual and practical success, knowing that God will establish our plans as we commit our work to Him.

Chapter 6
"Go Ye"

And Jesus came and spake unto them, saying, All power is given unto me in heaven and in earth. Go ye therefore, and teach all nations, baptizing them in the name of the Father, and of the Son, and of the Holy Ghost: teaching them to observe all things whatsoever I have commanded you: and, lo, I am with you always, even unto the end of the world. Amen.
—Matthew 28:18-20

I don't think that the entirety of scripture has been embraced, explored, and employed by the Church. When important parts are left out, they are overlooked, and unintended consequences occur. Whereas had we understood what was not embraced, it would lessen the possibility of the Church having to face it. The scripture above contains a huge benefit and assignment that was left out by the Church.

Matthew 28:18-19 is noted as the Great Commission to the Church. But this is not just a scriptural instruction to the institution arm that Believers frequent on weekends. Hearing, "Go ye," I wonder how we even missed the understanding, being you would have to "come ye" to the institution. This scripture is more importantly a commanding order to the organism arm of the Church. It ties back into why the Tower of Babel was an ungodly act. It was ungodly because they went up rather than going out. What most don't hear or see in "Go ye" is the restoration plan of God for the earth and the systems of the world. The reason we don't have a full grasp in our understanding here is because we cut short Jesus's statement of what the totality of preaching included.

Mark 1:14-15 – "Now after John was put in prison, Jesus came to Galilee, **preaching the Gospel of the Kingdom of God**, and saying, 'The time is fulfilled, and the Kingdom of God is at hand. Repent, and believe in the Gospel.'"

Matthew 10:7 – "And as you go, **preach**, saying, '**The Kingdom of Heaven** is at hand.'"

Luke 9:2 – "He sent them to **preach the Kingdom of God** and to heal the sick."

Matthew 24:14 – "And this **Gospel of the Kingdom will be preached** in all the world as a witness to all the nations, and then the end will come."

Jesus said go, and preach the **Gospel of the Kingdom of God**. The Kingdom of God being preached is not just Christ and His crucifixion for personal salvation, because Jesus did not just come for people. To only go for people leaves out the totality of Christ coming to earth. Jesus said to preach the Gospel of the Kingdom of God. The Gospel is a person. The Kingdom of God is an action empowered by the person of the Gospel, that manifests in lives and in environments the nature, character, and order of the person of the Gospel. The Gospel of the Kingdom of God is the reclaiming of people, places, and the things that were lost because of the fall of Adam. So the Kingdom of God (heaven's mode of operation—God's way of doing things) is what we take into the workforce, because with the Kingdom comes the power to be fruitful, multiply, replenish, subdue, have dominion, and conquer inside the kingdoms of this world. The Kingdom of God is also the working of spiritual principles that give the Believer an advantage in life. It's power from Heaven to produce change. Notice

> Many are so ready for Sunday to preach in the pulpit of an institution, not realizing that they step into their own pulpit every day when they enter the workspace.

that Matthew 24:14 said that the Gospel of the Kingdom will be preached in all the world **for a witness**.

For years, the Church has only witnessed about the person—Jesus—and neglected the witness that manifests as a result of the action: the marketplace. A witness is not just a talk about Jesus and the need for salvation. It is also what gives evidence to Jesus. A proof that is tangible and undeniable. Look at what Pharaoh said about Joseph and his God: **"Then Pharaoh said to Joseph, 'Since God has made all this known to you, there is no one so discerning and wise as you. You shall be in charge of my palace, and all my people are to submit to your orders'" (Gen. 41:39-40 NIV).** Pharaoh did not deny Joseph because he served a different God. Pharoah promoted Jospeh because he provided something that his own magicians and prophets couldn't—witness: **"Believe me when I say that I am in the Father and the Father is in me; or at least <u>believe on the evidence of the works themselves</u> (John 14:11 NIV).** The witness speaks of Jesus also—by providing incontestable fruit. This is what the Believer should be providing in the marketplace as they go—incontestable fruit.

Here is the point: The Kingdom of God has the answers and resolve that the world needs. It is an order to Believers to go into the world, not stand by and look at its demise. It's God's wish that none should perish. We should not be damming the world to hell. The "Go ye" is about bringing salvation to the world: **"The Lord is not slack concerning His promise, as some men count slackness; but is longsuffering to us-ward, not willing that any should perish, but that all should come to repentance" (II Pet. 3:9).**

Unfortunately, the Kingdom is not found positioned where it needs to be because Believers aren't going. The world needs answers from the Believers, while the Kingdom needs the actions of the Believer because in the Believer is where the Kingdom lies: **"Neither shall they say, Lo here! or, lo there! for, behold, <u>the Kingdom of God is within you"</u> (Luke 17:21)**. So, "Go ye," is more than what we have been taught—it's an answer. The world is in a world of problems, and God sends His Kingdom in us into the world to bring answers to the problems.

This is what it means to be Kingdom-minded. Have you ever considered that answers save? The marketplace is the biggest mission field, and Believers are there every single day and yet miss the Kingdom of God being preached. Many are so ready for Sunday to preach in the pulpit of an institution, not realizing that they step into a pulpit every day when they enter the workspace. The same with the use of gifts, when right there in the marketplace are lives waiting to have an encounter with God. Your career is one of the greatest mission fields. You have the ability to put Christ on display every day and get rewarded for it all at the same time.

Permission Granted

There is a belief that has gotten into the minds of Believers that has caused a tremendous stagnation in Believers' success, almost to the degree that success is seen as being evil.

It is believed that any actionable step a Believer takes is not of God unless God has said that they could. I do not fully agree with this train of thought. Without having proper context, many Believers have suffered and missed amazing opportunities for promotion and doors that were open to favor them. If God gives every man spiritual gifts, special talents, and acquired skills, at the very least, with those come an identifiable action step. Just simply look at what the gift, talent, or skill does or how it works, and there you have it—your Word/permission from God. That information in and of itself is enough to get started. It rules out having to sit still and wonder what's next. Get active in what it first revealed. What does the talent do? What are you skilled at? If you can answer these questions, you have found what you are permitted to do. And as you progress in doing that, God can give more detail and further instruction—while you're on your way. But most Believers are looking for the full

> God meets you and directs you to step, not stand still.

details, when you simply need to get started. Put the gift, talent, or skill to work, in the environment it is created in or with the thing it is created to work on, and you will begin to see the specifics of exactly what you are to do. **"Whatsoever thy hand findeth to do, do it with thy might" (Ecc. 9:10a).**

You already have permission! Gifts, talents, skills, and abilities weren't given to lie dormant—put them to work. The entire fabric of this book lands on Luke 19:13 (NIV): "So he called ten of his servants and gave them ten minas. **'<u>Put this money to work</u>,' he said, 'until I come back."** What else did they need to hear? The nobleman said, "Put what you have to work." He not only got instruction on what to do but how long to do it: "until I come back." And so I say to you what the nobleman said to them—**put it to work!** You have permission. God doesn't have anything to say right now because you aren't moving or working with what you currently have.

The scripture I'm about to share is loaded. It provides so much peace and assurance. But I used to read this scripture through a religious lens, and it kept me from doing anything until I heard God. My thinking was limited, and became that way because I was taught to think this way. I don't want you to walk in limit:

> **For this cause we also, since the day we heard it, do not cease to pray for you, and to desire that ye might be filled with the knowledge of His will in all wisdom and spiritual understanding; that ye might walk worthy of the Lord unto all pleasing, being fruitful in every good work, and increasing in the knowledge of God; strengthened with all might, according to His glorious power, unto all patience and longsuffering with joyfulness; giving thanks unto the Father, which hath made us meet to be partakers of the inheritance of the saints in light (Col. 1:9-12).**

We are in danger when we lack the desire to be filled with the full knowledge of His will, which makes us partakers of the inheritance.

I read this verse one day and heard what I thought I needed to wait on God to say: **"<u>The steps</u> of good man are ordered by the Lord: and He delighteth in his way" (Ps. 37:23)**. I was sitting there knowing my potential and abilities, but I believed that I couldn't move because I hadn't heard God tell me what to do next. And He'd already spoken. It was right there all the time—**the steps are ordered**. God meets you, and directs stepping, not standing still. I didn't have any steps. God had no place to meet me, nor did He have any steps to order/direct because I wasn't taking any. You have got to take the step!

Why aren't you moving? Permission has been granted. Abilities have been given to you, and you are standing still. So, you say, but where? Easy. Put them where they have been meant and made to work. The one-talent servant lost what he had because he did nothing with his talent. He was chastised <u>for not putting the talent in an environment where the talent could work</u>, so that at the very least it could have yielded some interest. God does not give you anything with an expectation of it remaining the same once it's in your hands, because remember, your hands are anointed to prosper: **"Go to the ant, thou sluggard; consider her ways, and be wise: which having no guide, overseer, or ruler, provideth her meat in the summer, and gathereth her food in the harvest. How long wilt thou sleep, O sluggard? when wilt thou arise out of thy sleep? Yet a little sleep, a little slumber, a little folding of the hands to sleep: so shall thy poverty come as one that travelleth, and thy want as an armed man. (Prov. 6:6-11).**

Kingdom Impact

The world is in a broken, chaotic state. Post-COVID, nothing seems to be the same. The character of business and customer service has drastically diminished. Many businesses, once known for their commitment to excellence, have lowered their standards in favor of efficiency, quick profits, or simply surviving in a challenging economic climate. As companies struggle to maintain quality and integrity, trust between consumers and businesses has eroded. The marketplace has become more transactional and less relational, with customer service often an afterthought rather than a priority.

But in what seems like a train wreck lies the perfect opportunity for the Kingdom of God to shine. In the midst of this chaos, there is a divine opening for Believers to step into the marketplace with a higher standard—bringing Kingdom principles of excellence, integrity, and service into the world of business. This is where the body of Christ can make its mark, reflecting the character of God by delivering work and service that honor Him.

Romans 8:19 tells us, **"For the creation waits in eager expectation for the children of God to be revealed."** The world is desperate for something better—for businesses that not only meet needs but also exceed expectations, for leaders who value people over profits, and for organizations that operate with integrity and compassion. The earth even knows that its current condition is opposed to its natural functionality and can be corrected by the sons of God—Kingdom-preneurs. The problem is that Believers aren't aware that this is a part of the assignment if the Church and that correcting these things are directly connected to marketplace ministry. Now, more than ever, there is a hunger for what the Kingdom of God has to offer. And God has placed Believers strategically in the marketplace to meet this need.

The chaos and brokenness of the post-COVID world create a prime opportunity for Christians to stand out by upholding Kingdom values. While others may cut corners or settle for mediocrity, Believers can rise above and show that there is a better way—a way that reflects the excellence, compassion, and integrity of Christ. **Colossians 3:17** instructs us, "And whatever you do, whether in word or deed, do it all in the name of the Lord Jesus, giving thanks to God the Father through Him." This scripture challenges us to maintain a Kingdom standard in all that we do, especially in business, where our actions speak louder than words.

This is the moment for Kingdom-minded businesspeople to restore the broken systems of the world by creating businesses that not only provide goods and services but also restore dignity, trust, and value to the marketplace. In a world that is used to poor customer service, lack of integrity, and broken promises, businesses led by Kingdom principles can become beacons of hope. Imagine businesses where every product is crafted with care, every service is delivered with a genuine heart, and every transaction reflects the Kingdom of God.

The Kingdom of God thrives in places where the world is lacking.

This is not a utopian dream; it's a reality that can be achieved when Believers take their place in the marketplace and do business God's way. Proverbs 22:29 NIV says, **"Do you see someone skilled in their work? They will serve before kings; they will not serve before officials of low rank."** This verse highlights the power of skill, excellence, and diligence. As Believers, we are called to be skilled and excellent in our work, and when we uphold this standard, it opens doors for influence, even before the highest authorities. Excellence, in the context of Kingdom business, is not just about being the best, it's about reflecting the nature of God in everything we do. It's about showing the world that our work reflects the Creator and that through our work, we honor Him. Moreover, in a world where ethical business practices seem to be diminishing, integrity becomes a powerful tool for Kingdom advancement. Proverbs 11:3 NLT reminds us, **"Honesty guides good people; dishonesty destroys treacherous people."** Integrity in business sets Believers apart. When we are honest, transparent, and trustworthy, we gain the respect and trust of those we serve. This is how we build long-term relationships, not just short-term profits. By being people of integrity, we embody the values of the Kingdom and create a platform for others to see Christ through us.

The post-COVID era may be marked by uncertainty, but it is also marked by opportunity. The Kingdom of God thrives in places where the world is lacking. Where there is chaos, we bring order. Where there is dishonesty, we bring truth. Where there is mediocrity, we bring excellence. The marketplace is ripe for this kind of transformation, and it will happen through Believers who are willing to step into their God-given roles as business leaders, entrepreneurs, and employees who operate with Kingdom values. In this new era, the world is watching. People are looking for businesses they can trust, leaders they can rely on, and products and services that reflect care and quality. This is where the Church has the chance to make a lasting impact. By doing business God's way, using the gifts He has given us, rooted in His Word, and empowered by His Spirit, we can show the world that there is a better way to operate. We can demonstrate that even in business, the Kingdom of God is active, powerful, and transformative. And as we do, we fulfill Jesus's command to "do business until He comes," allowing His Kingdom to expand through every area of the marketplace.

Chapter 7
Kingdom-preneur

Who hath saved us, and called us with an holy calling, not according to our works, but according to his own purpose and grace, which was given us in Christ Jesus before the world began,
—II Timothy 1:9

Kingdom-preneur has to do with one's calling to purpose and where the gift is assigned to work and function. Adam was created as an employee of the Kingdom of God. The calling for his purpose was to be fruitful, multiply, replenish, subdue, and have dominion. But none of this would be done inside of a building. This calling would happen throughout the earth, which means we would see Adam living out his purpose amongst us. **God's people are called to make a difference in the world through their work**. I want to show you the Kingdom-preneurs in the Bible:

Abraham – A Wealthy Livestock Owner and Landowner

Abraham, a successful herdsman and landowner, was called by God to establish a covenant that would bless all nations. His obedience to leave his homeland and prosper in a foreign land allowed him to be a key figure in God's plan to establish a people set apart for Him. Abraham's business dealings, wealth, and interactions with local kings (Gen. 14) showed how God's favor positioned him to influence others. Abraham's wealth and success weren't just for personal gain.

God used him to bless nations, illustrating how marketplace influence can open doors for divine purposes.

Isaac – A Successful Farmer and Well Digger

Isaac, like his father Abraham, was a businessman who excelled in agriculture and land management. His prosperity became a testament to God's blessing. Even amidst conflict with the Philistines, Isaac persisted in digging wells, securing vital resources for his community. Isaac's success in the marketplace made him a powerful figure in the region, and his reliance on God for favor and provision demonstrated how God can prosper those who trust in Him while working in secular fields.

Jacob – A Livestock Breeder and Entrepreneur

Jacob's innovative business practices with livestock (Gen. 30:31-43) allowed him to build great wealth despite working under Laban's oppressive conditions. God gave him supernatural insight into breeding techniques that allowed him to flourish. Jacob's entrepreneurial spirit and strategic thinking helped him become the father of the twelve tribes of Israel, playing a pivotal role in the nation God was building through him.

Joseph – A Government Official and Marketplace Administrator

Joseph's role as the governor of Egypt allowed him to not only save his family from famine but also manage Egypt's economy with divine wisdom. His position enabled him to influence the entire region, and his integrity in the marketplace preserved God's people. Joseph's elevation in a secular environment led to the fulfillment of God's promise to Abraham. His wisdom in the marketplace was instrumental in preserving the lineage through which the Messiah would come.

Daniel – A High-Ranking Government Official in Babylon

Daniel worked in a pagan government yet maintained his loyalty to God. His wisdom, integrity, and ability to interpret dreams earned him high positions under several kings. Even in captivity, Daniel's influence shaped policies and brought God's agenda to a foreign land. Through Daniel's leadership, God's wisdom was introduced into the heart of the most powerful empire of the time, demonstrating how God can use His people in secular positions to advance His plans.

King Solomon – A Wealthy King and Business Magnate

Solomon was not only a king but also a businessman who traded extensively with other nations. His wealth and wisdom were unparalleled, and his influence reached far beyond Israel. Leaders from around the world sought his counsel. Solomon's success in business and governance led to the expansion of Israel's influence, and his wisdom pointed others to God as the source of all knowledge and understanding.

Jesus – A Carpenter Turned Savior of the World

Before beginning His public ministry, Jesus worked as a carpenter, engaging in a profession that served the community. His time in this trade shows that work, even seemingly ordinary work, is valuable in the eyes of God. Jesus's time as a carpenter prepared Him for His public ministry. He understood the challenges of daily life, making His teachings relatable to the everyday person. His humble background elevated the dignity of all work and showed that God values all kinds of professions in advancing His Kingdom.

The Woman with the Oil – A Resourceful Entrepreneur

This widow faced a financial crisis and was at risk of losing her sons to slavery. When she sought help from Elisha, he instructed her to gather jars and fill them with the little oil she had left. Miraculously, the oil kept flowing, and she was able to sell it, pay her debts, and live off the surplus. Her oil business became the means through which God provided for her family, showing that God can use even the smallest resources to create wealth and sustain His people. This story underscores the principle that God empowers His people to use the resources at hand to solve problems and advance His provision.

Each of these figures had occupations outside of the religious or "church" setting, yet their marketplace roles were instrumental in advancing God's agenda. Whether through livestock, government, carpentry, or entrepreneurship, these individuals were empowered by God to influence their spheres and bring His Kingdom purposes to fruition. They demonstrate that Kingdom-preneurs, empowered by God, can transform the world not just within the Church, but especially in the marketplace.

When a Believer in business grasps the reality that they are not just entrepreneurs but are, in fact, Kingdom-preneurs, employed by God to further His purposes in the marketplace, the benefits are vast and profound. This understanding shifts their approach to business from a purely transactional endeavor to a divinely empowered mission. One of the greatest advantages of being a Kingdom-preneur is the ability to tap into divine wisdom: **"If any of you lack wisdom, let him ask of God, that giveth to all men liberally, and upbraideth not; and it shall be given him" (James 1:5)**. As a Kingdom-preneur, you have access to God's guidance in making critical business decisions. When others may rely solely on human strategy and insight, you can lean on supernatural wisdom, gaining insights that position you ahead of the competition. This divine insight isn't limited to business operations alone. It extends to foresight about market trends, potential opportunities, and even risks to avoid: **"Howbeit when He, the Spirit of truth, is come, He will guide you into all truth: for He shall not speak of Himself; but whatsoever He shall hear, that shall He speak: and He will shew you things to come" (John 16:13)**. Holy Spirit becomes your business consultant, giving you access to knowledge beyond your natural capabilities.

> As ambassadors of Christ, you carry the authority of Heaven into every business interaction, boardroom, and deal.

When you understand that you are employed by God as His Kingdom-preneur, you recognize that your provision comes from Him. This shifts the pressure off of you and places it on God's covenant to provide: **"But remember the Lord your God, for it is He who gives you the ability to produce wealth" (Deut. 8:18 NIV).** God's favor can open doors that no amount of networking or effort could unlock. This favor can manifest in contracts, clients, and partnerships that seemingly come out of nowhere. Psalm 5:12 (NIV) says, "Surely, Lord, you bless the righteous; you surround them with your favor as with a shield." When you walk in divine favor, what would take others years to achieve can happen for you in a fraction of the time, because God accelerates your success according to His purposes.

While others in business may be focused solely on profits, Kingdom-preneurs understand that their work has eternal significance. When you view your business as a platform for advancing God's Kingdom, your goals transcend financial success. Your business becomes a tool for impacting lives, advancing God's principles, and serving others with excellence and integrity. This eternal perspective infuses your work with deeper meaning and purpose. It compels you to operate with integrity, knowing that your ultimate employer is God, and your rewards are both earthly and eternal. **"Rendering service readily with goodwill, as to the Lord and not to men, Knowing that for whatever good anyone does, he will receive his reward from the Lord, whether he is slave or free (Eph. 6:7-8 AMPC)**.

> As a Kingdom-preneur, you are not limited by earthly resources.

Kingdom-preneurs are uniquely empowered to bring about change. As ambassadors of Christ, you carry the authority of Heaven into every business interaction, boardroom, and deal. The marketplace is one of the largest mission fields, and when you operate with a Kingdom mindset, you influence the culture and dynamics of your industry. As you model Christ-like character, others will take notice. This influence can lead to an environment where God's values are reflected in how business is conducted, creating a ripple effect that touches employees, clients, and competitors alike. When you operate from a place of humility, service, and trust in God's timing, your business gains a firm foundation that can withstand economic downturns, market fluctuations, and other challenges. The world's model of success is often built on competition, self-interest, and short-term gain. However, a Kingdom-preneur operates with Kingdom principles that lead to lasting, sustainable success: **"Humility is the fear of the Lord; its wages are riches and honor and life" (Prov. 22:4 NIV)**. Kingdom-preneurs also understand the importance of sowing and reaping: **"Give, and it will be given to you. A good measure, pressed down, shaken together and running over, will be poured into your lap" (Luke 6:38 NIV).** This law of generosity ensures that Kingdom-preneurs not only receive financial returns but also experience the overflow of resources—financial, relational, and spiritual.

One of the most overlooked benefits of being a Kingdom-preneur is the divine protection that comes with aligning your business with God's purposes: **"Whoever dwells in the shelter of the Most High will rest in the shadow of the Almighty" (Ps. 91:1 NIV).** When your business is under the Lordship of Christ, you can trust Him to protect your endeavors from harm, whether that be attacks from competitors, economic instability, or personal burnout. Moreover, as a Kingdom-preneur, you can operate from a place of peace: **"Do not be anxious about anything, but in every situation, by prayer and petition, with thanksgiving, present your requests to God. And the peace of God, which transcends all understanding, will guard your hearts and your minds in Christ Jesus" (Philippians 4:6-7 NIV).** Instead of living with the constant stress and anxiety that plagues many business owners, you can rest in the peace that comes from knowing your business is in God's hands. As a Kingdom-preneur, you are not limited by earthly resources. This means that the success of your business is not determined by the state of the global economy, but by God's limitless supply. When you understand that God is your source, you are free from the fear of lack. You can make bold, faith-driven decisions, knowing that Heaven's resources are available to back you up. This allows you to be more generous, invest in others, and expand your business without being bound by a scarcity mentality.

Finally, a Kingdom-preneur leaves a legacy that extends far beyond wealth or accolades. **"A good person leaves an inheritance for their children's children" (Prov. 13:22 NIV).** By operating your business according to Kingdom principles, you not only create wealth that can be passed down, but you also leave a legacy of righteousness, integrity, and faith for generations to come. This legacy is not just financial, but spiritual. Those who work with or for you will witness the example of someone who lives out their faith in the marketplace, and that influence can extend into the lives of employees, partners, and even clients, pointing them toward Christ.

When you understand that you are not just a businessperson but a Kingdom-preneur employed by God, the benefits are extraordinary. From divine wisdom and supernatural provision to marketplace transformation and eternal impact, your business becomes more than a means to make a living; it becomes a tool for Kingdom advancement. By trusting in God's power and provision, you position yourself to operate in His abundance, favor, and protection, leaving a lasting legacy that extends beyond the marketplace into eternity.

Creating a Kingdom Culture

In today's business world, the culture of a company plays a significant role in its success. It shapes how employees interact, how decisions are made, and how customers experience the business. For Christian entrepreneurs and leaders, creating a Kingdom culture in business is not just an option but a mandate. I made the decision to create a Kingdom culture in my business when I opened it. And to this very day, when I come across old customers, they tell me how much they appreciated a shop that had the type of environment we presented. And I can bear witness to the fact that the environment we created compelled our clients to tip more. Christians do not have to be in fear of creating a kingdom culture in their establishment or in how they do business. The Kingdom culture is a culture of giving the best, doing the best, and going over and above.

A Kingdom culture is one that reflects the values, principles, and heart of God's Kingdom in every aspect of the business, from the way people are treated to the integrity of its operations. A Kingdom culture in business is a Christ-centered approach to creating an environment where biblical principles are lived out daily. It goes beyond merely having Christian values written on a wall or in a mission statement. It involves actively cultivating a workplace atmosphere where people feel valued, integrity is upheld, excellence is pursued, and the company operates as a steward of both resources and relationships. Jesus said in Matthew 6:33, **"But seek ye first the kingdom of God, and His righteousness; and all these things shall be added unto you."** When a business seeks first the Kingdom of God, its culture reflects the characteristics of the Kingdom: righteousness, peace, joy, integrity, love, and justice. Creating such a culture doesn't just benefit the business; it transforms the lives of employees, customers, and the community, making the business a beacon of light in the marketplace.

One of the cornerstones of a Kingdom culture is the pursuit of excellence in all things. This is rooted in biblical principles. There should never be a question of what you will get when a Believer is leading, or you go to the establishment of a Believer. If it God's desire that we have the best, then it should be our desire to always give our best—in whatever we do, especially in business. In a Kingdom-driven business, every task, product, and service is completed with the mindset that it is ultimately for God's glory. In a Kingdom culture, ethical behavior and honesty are non-negotiable. Employees and leaders are encouraged to act with transparency, fairness, and righteousness, knowing that God blesses those who walk in integrity.

In many businesses, profits are the primary focus, often at the expense of employees' well-being. However, in a Kingdom culture, people are valued over profits. This doesn't mean that financial success is neglected, but rather that the business prioritizes the health, development, and flourishing of its employees and customers. Jesus demonstrated this principle in how He treated people. He saw their inherent value, even when the world overlooked them. Philippians 2:4 AMPC says, **"Let each of you esteem and look upon and be concerned for not [merely] his own interests, but also each for the interests of others."** A Kingdom culture encourages servant leadership, where leaders exist to serve their employees and foster an environment where everyone can thrive.

Businesses with a Kingdom culture will invest in the growth and development of their employees, offering opportunities for learning, mentorship, and personal growth. **"Let no one then seek his own good and advantage and profit, but [rather] each one of the other [let him seek the welfare of his neighbor]" (I Cor. 10:24 AMPC)**. Employees are not just viewed as a means to an end but as individuals made in the image of God, each with unique gifts and potential. When people feel valued, they are more engaged, more loyal, and more committed to the success of the business. The reason why we need the Kingdom in the marketplace is because in a Kingdom culture, collaboration is promoted over competition and unity over division. In the Bible, First Corinthians 12:12 teaches us that the body of Christ is made up of many parts, each contributing uniquely to the whole. Similarly, in a business with a Kingdom culture, employees are encouraged to collaborate, understanding that collective effort is more powerful than individual performance. This culture of collaboration breaks down silos within organizations and fosters open communication and mutual respect. Employees are seen as vital contributors to the company's mission and vision, rather than mere cogs in a machine. By working together, the team can achieve more and create a sense of shared purpose, which strengthens the overall culture.

> Believers are called not only to participate in culture but to lead and shape it.

A Kingdom culture is outward-focused, understanding that the business exists not just to make money but to make a positive impact on the world. This reflects the biblical principle of stewardship, where businesses recognize that they are entrusted with resources not just for their own benefit but for the good of others. Proverbs 19:17 says, **"He that hath pity upon the poor lendeth unto the Lord; and that which he hath given will He pay him again."** Businesses with a Kingdom mindset look for ways to serve their local communities, whether through charitable giving, volunteerism, or creating initiatives that address societal needs like poverty, education, or healthcare. This not only aligns with Kingdom values but also enhances the reputation of the business, building trust and loyalty with customers and stakeholders.

There are some practical things you can do in your business to establish a Kingdom culture and provide service that characterizes a culture influenced by the Kingdom of God.

1. **Define and communicate core values** - Every business with a Kingdom culture must clearly define its core values. These values should be rooted in biblical principles such as integrity, service, stewardship, and excellence. Once defined, these values must be communicated clearly and regularly to both employees and customers. Values shouldn't just be theoretical—they should be visible in the way the company operates on a daily basis.
2. **Model kingdom leadership** - Leadership sets the tone for the entire organization. Leaders in a Kingdom culture must lead by example, demonstrating the values of humility, service, and integrity. Mark 10:43-45 teaches us that the greatest leaders are those who serve others. By modeling servant leadership, business leaders can inspire their teams to follow suit and foster a culture of mutual respect and service.
3. **Prioritize employee development** - Investing in employees is key to establishing a Kingdom culture. Offer opportunities for personal and professional growth through mentorship programs, training, and open feedback loops. When employees know that their development is a priority, they feel valued and are more likely to contribute positively to the business's mission.

4. **Encourage accountability and integrity** – Creating a Kingdom culture requires accountability. Set up structures that ensure ethical practices and integrity are maintained at every level of the business. Foster an environment where employees can speak up if something isn't right, knowing that the leadership will respond with fairness and integrity. This level of accountability helps sustain a Kingdom culture over the long term.

5. **Engage in community outreach** – A business with a Kingdom culture seeks to serve the broader community. This could be through financial support to charitable causes, employee volunteer programs, or creating products and services that address societal challenges. The goal is to reflect the heart of God in all interactions, not just within the business, but in the impact it has on the world around it.

Creating a Kingdom culture in business not only enhances the internal dynamics of the company but also influences the broader marketplace. Businesses that prioritize values over profits, serve their communities, and operate with integrity become beacons of light in industries where ethics are often compromised. Over time, these businesses stand out, attract loyal customers, and build long-term success. A Kingdom culture reflects God's character in the business world. It transforms not only the business itself but the lives of employees, customers, and the community, demonstrating that businesses built on biblical principles can thrive while advancing God's Kingdom.

When Believers take the lead in business, education, and media, they are not just fulfilling their personal ambitions—they are positioning themselves to **infuse Kingdom values into cultural systems**. The impact of having a Christian in a decision-making seat can be profound because their decisions affect not only their immediate organization but also set new standards for industries, communities, and society as a whole.

Kingdom leadership brings a higher standard of ethics and compassion into industries. For example, in business, Kingdom leaders can drive the adoption of ethical practices that prioritize people over profit. In education, they can influence policies and curricula that foster holistic development and prepare students to lead with integrity. In media, they can tell stories that inspire change and bring attention to issues that matter, framing them through a lens of hope and redemption.

Believers are called not only to participate in the culture but to lead and shape it. When Christians occupy seats of authority in business, education, and media, they bring Kingdom values to places that desperately need transformation. This is a call for Christians to aspire to leadership roles, recognizing that their influence extends far beyond their personal success. By aiming for these positions, they can advance the Kingdom agenda and set new cultural norms that reflect the principles of heaven. Be bold in believing for positions of influence and trust that God can use you to bring significant cultural change. Your leadership can create environments where justice, truth, and compassion prevail, making a lasting impact that extends far beyond your lifetime.

Balanced in Business

For Christian leaders, work without rest can also reflect a deeper issue of misplaced trust.

For Kingdom business leaders, maintaining a healthy work-life balance and prioritizing rest are critical not only to personal well-being but also to effective leadership. In a fast-paced world that often glorifies overwork and constant hustle, many business leaders, including Christians, fall into the trap of neglecting rest and other important aspects of their lives. However, the Bible provides a different model, one that emphasizes the value of rest, stewardship of time, and living in balance as essential components of a Kingdom-centered life.

The importance of rest is woven throughout scripture, beginning with the creation story. Genesis 2:2-3 shows us that even God, after creating the heavens and the earth, rested on the seventh day: **"And**

on the seventh day God ended His work which He had made; and He rested on the seventh day from all His work which He had made. And God blessed the seventh day, and sanctified it." God didn't need rest because He was tired, but He modeled the principle of rest for humanity. This act of resting after work reflects a divine rhythm of labor and renewal that we are called to follow.

The concept of Sabbath rest was later formalized in the Ten Commandments, as Exodus 20:8-10 commands, **"Remember the sabbath day, to keep it holy. Six days shalt thou labour, and do all thy work: But the seventh day is the sabbath of the Lord thy God: in it thou shalt not do any work."** Sabbath is not merely about taking a break from work; it is a spiritual practice that involves trusting God's provision, reflecting on His goodness, and resetting our physical, emotional, and spiritual well-being.

As Kingdom business leaders, we are called to follow this example. Rest is not a sign of weakness or inefficiency; it is a gift from God and a crucial element of maintaining balance, perspective, and effectiveness in both business and life. In today's competitive marketplace, many leaders feel pressure to work longer hours, sacrifice personal time, and push harder in order to stay ahead. While hard work and diligence are important qualities, the Bible warns us about the dangers of overworking and neglecting the need for rest. Ecclesiastes 4:6 says, **"Better is a handful with quietness, than both the hands full with travail and vexation of spirit."** This verse reminds us that a life of constant work without balance leads to burnout and frustration. When leaders neglect rest, they can quickly lose clarity, creativity, and even physical health, which ultimately diminishes their ability to lead effectively. Furthermore, overworking can cause strain on relationships with family, friends, and even God, as leaders become consumed with their professional responsibilities at the expense of personal and spiritual growth.

> A well-rested leader is more creative, more discerning, and better equipped to handle challenges with wisdom and clarity.

For Christian leaders, work without rest can also reflect a deeper issue of misplaced trust. Psalm 127:1-2 states, **"Except the Lord build the house, they labour in vain that build it: except the Lord keep the city, the watchman waketh but in vain. It is vain for you to rise up early, to sit up late, to eat the bread of sorrows: for so He giveth His beloved sleep."** This passage teaches us that working excessively, without taking time to rest, implies that we are depending solely on our own efforts rather than trusting God to provide. Rest allows us to acknowledge that God is in control, even when we are not working.

Kingdom leadership involves good stewardship of all resources, including time. Balancing work with rest and personal life is part of being a wise steward of the time God has given us. Just as we manage finances and other resources, we are called to manage our time in a way that reflects God's order and purpose for our lives. Ephesians 5:15-17 encourages Believers to **"be very careful, then, how you live—not as unwise but as wise, making the most of every opportunity, because the days are evil. Therefore do not be foolish, but understand what the Lord's will is."** This involves making intentional decisions about how we spend our time, balancing our professional responsibilities with time for God, family, and personal renewal. For the Kingdom business leader, this balance is not just about achieving personal well-being; it is about modeling a life of faith and trust in God to those we lead. By prioritizing rest and maintaining healthy boundaries, we demonstrate that we are dependent on God's provision rather than our own abilities, which speaks volumes in a culture that often idolizes work.

Rest is not just about physical recovery; it also restores our mental, emotional, and spiritual health. A well-rested leader is more creative, more discerning, and better equipped to handle challenges with wisdom and clarity. Rest allows leaders to recharge, gain new perspectives, and return to their work with renewed energy and vision. Jesus Himself modeled the importance of rest throughout His ministry. In the Gospels, we often see Jesus withdrawing from the crowds to find solitude and pray. Mark 6:31 says, **"And He said unto**

them, Come ye yourselves apart into a desert place, and rest a while: for there were many coming and going, and they had no leisure so much as to eat." Even in the midst of a busy ministry, Jesus made rest a priority for both Himself and His disciples. He knew that rest was essential for sustaining the effectiveness of His work.

For Kingdom business leaders, making time for rest and reflection is not only beneficial for personal health but also enhances leadership effectiveness. By stepping away from the daily grind, leaders can gain clarity about long-term goals, hear from God regarding the direction of the business, and avoid burnout. You have a work life, but you also need rest.

1. **Schedule regular times of rest** - Just as you would schedule important meetings or deadlines, intentionally schedule times of rest. This could include taking a Sabbath day each week, planning regular vacations, or simply setting aside time daily for personal renewal and prayer. These times should be sacred and not easily interrupted by work demands.

2. **Delegate and trust your team** - Effective delegation is key to maintaining work-life balance. As a leader, learn to trust your team and empower them to take on responsibilities. This not only gives you the opportunity to rest but also helps develop your team's skills and leadership capabilities.

3. **Set boundaries for work and personal life** - Establish clear boundaries between work and personal life. Avoid bringing work home or being constantly available outside of working hours. By setting boundaries, you protect your personal time and prevent burnout.

4. **Spend time in prayer and reflection** - Incorporate regular times of prayer and reflection into your routine. This not only helps you stay spiritually grounded but also allows you to seek God's wisdom for your work and life. Prayer is a form of rest for the soul, and it rejuvenates you in ways that physical rest cannot.

Work-life balance and rest are not just luxuries; they are necessities for the Kingdom business leader. God has given us the gift of rest as a way to rejuvenate our bodies, minds, and spirits, enabling us to lead with clarity, creativity, and compassion. By modeling a life of balance and trust in God, Kingdom leaders not only sustain their personal well-being but also demonstrate the principles of faith and stewardship to those they lead. Rest is a powerful reminder that success in the marketplace ultimately comes from God's provision, and not from our constant striving. As Kingdom business leaders, embracing rest is part of honoring God with our work and our lives.

Chapter 8

Do Business

He said therefore, A certain man of birth went on to a far country, to take to himself a kingdom, and to return, 13 And having called ten servants of his own, he gave to them ten pounds, and said unto them, Do business—till I come.

—Luke 19:12-13YLT

AKJV – **Occupy** till I come.
AMPC – **Buy and sell** with these while I go and then return.
MSG – "**Operate with this** until I return."
NIV – **"Put this money to work,"** he said, "until I come back."
NLT – **Invest this** for me while I am gone.

This command to **do business** is no less than any other command. And notice that it came from Jesus Christ Himself. This command to "do business" is not simply about financial transactions but represents the larger call of the Church to occupy, engage, and expand the Kingdom of God in the world, particularly in the marketplace.

Jesus, as the Master in the parable, gives His followers clear instructions to be active in the world, using their gifts, resources, and influence to further His Kingdom. The marketplace, where business, culture, and society intersect, is a primary area where this mandate is fulfilled. This chapter will explore how the Church is called to "do business" in the marketplace, demonstrating the Kingdom of God through the Word of God and through the unique gifts that Believers have been given. From the very beginning, God intended for His people to have influence and dominion over the earth. In Genesis 1:28, God commands Adam and Eve, **"Be fruitful and multiply, and fill the earth and subdue it; have dominion over the fish of the sea, over the birds of the air, and over every living thing that moves on the earth."** This original mandate included both spiritual and practical leadership in the world. Today, one of the primary spheres where Believers are called to exercise this dominion is the marketplace.

The marketplace is not merely a place of commerce but a mission field where the Kingdom of God is to be displayed and expanded. Believers are called to bring the light of Christ into the economic, social, and cultural systems of the world, transforming them with the values of the Kingdom. The Church is called to be a visible, transformative presence in the marketplace. By "doing business" with excellence, integrity, and faith, Believers demonstrate the power and reality of the Kingdom of God to the world. The workplace, the boardroom, and the marketplace are all areas where the Church is meant to be active, showing forth the glory of God through skill, creativity, and leadership.

> The marketplace is one of the most powerful arenas for Believers to display their God-given gifts.

Marketplace ministry is not a secondary calling; it is integral to the mission of the Church. Throughout scripture, God placed His people in strategic positions of influence within the marketplace. The Bible is filled with examples of men and women of faith who impacted nations through their business dealings and leadership. Joseph, as we saw earlier, was elevated to the position of managing all the resources of Egypt (Gen. 41:41-43). Daniel served in the courts of Babylon, leading with such integrity and excellence that he gained influence with multiple kings. His work as a government official was a form of marketplace ministry, showing that Believers could serve faithfully in secular systems while remaining committed to God's purposes (Dan. 6:3). His influence in the marketplace led to the acknowledgment of God's power in a pagan nation. In the New Testament, we also see examples of business leaders like Lydia, a seller of purple cloth (Acts 16:14). Lydia was not only a successful entrepreneur but also an early supporter of Paul's ministry. Her business provided her with the resources to host gatherings of Believers in her home, expanding the reach of the Gospel. These biblical examples reveal that God places His people in positions of influence within the marketplace to demonstrate the principles of His Kingdom. The Church's role in the marketplace is not just about evangelism, but about transforming the systems of the world to reflect Kingdom values such as justice, righteousness, generosity, and love.

Activating Gifts in the Marketplace

Each of you should use whatever gift you have received to serve others, as faithful stewards of God's grace in its various forms.
—I Peter 4:10

The Church's role in the marketplace is importantly powerful because Believers need to be equipped on how to use their spiritual gifts to bring about life transformation. Whether in business, education, government, or the arts, the Believer's gift can work. The Church must teach and encourage Believers to base their business practices and leadership on the principles found in the Word of God.

The Bible provides wisdom for every aspect of life, including work and commerce. Proverbs 3:5-6 NLT reminds us to **"trust in the Lord with all your heart; do not depend on your own understanding. Seek his will in all you do, and he will show you which path to take."** By aligning business practices with biblical principles, the Church can help Believers navigate the complexities of the marketplace with wisdom and integrity. Whether through creativity, leadership, innovation, or problem-solving, Believers are called to shine in their respective industries.

The marketplace is one of the most powerful arenas for Believers to display their God-given gifts. When Believers apply their gifts in the marketplace, they bring the influence of the Kingdom to bear in ways that can transform businesses, industries, and communities. We have said this before, but it is worth saying again: the Church must also encourage Believers to demonstrate the values of the Kingdom in their work. Colossians 3:23 says, **"Whatever you do, work at it with all your heart, as working for the Lord, not for human masters."** Without question, there should be an expectation of nothing less than timeliness, cleanliness, excellence, integrity, character, diligence, and superb proficiency from the Believer in the marketplace. You are not called to fit in—you are called to stand out: **"Exhort servants to be obedient unto their own masters, and to please them well in all things; not answering again" (Tit. 2:9-10).**

The command to "do business until I come" is a direct call to the Church to be active in the world. The Church is not called to retreat from the marketplace, but to engage with it fully, bringing the light and power of the Kingdom of God into every industry. This call is not limited to pastors or ministry leaders; every Believer, whether they are in business, education, technology, or the arts, is called to "do business" with a Kingdom mindset. We are stewards of the gifts and resources God has given us, and He expects us to multiply them. Whether through entrepreneurship, innovation, or faithful leadership, Believers are called to expand their influence and make an impact for the Kingdom in the marketplace.

> Jesus gave use the institution for learning and the world to the organism for ministering.

The marketplace is a mission field where God is calling His people to step up, activate their gifts, and bring Kingdom solutions to the challenges of the world. By aligning their work with God's Word and operating under the anointing of the Holy Spirit, Believers can fulfill the command of Jesus to "do business" until He comes, bringing glory to God and expanding His Kingdom on earth.

The Church is not just called to the four walls of a building but is commissioned to be active in the marketplace. The command to "do business" until Jesus returns is a mandate for Believers to take their place in the world, using their gifts and talents to demonstrate the reality of the Kingdom of God. The Church should be a force to reckon within the marketplace, because Believers bring to that world something that that world does not have: Jesus—the All-Wise, All-Knowing, and All-Sufficient One. We aren't just saved—we bring salvation, for the Lord has commanded us, saying, **"I have made you a light for the Gentiles, that you may bring salvation to the ends of the earth" (Acts 13:47 ESV).** Believers should bring into business a wisdom and knowledge that only God can give and is superior to any wisdom of man. The skillset of a Believer should exceed that of the world because Believers have the help and aid of the Holy Spirit coupled with the anointing that destroys yokes and removes burdens. Through business, leadership, creativity, and integrity, the Church has the opportunity to transform industries and impact society in profound ways.

> Believers are called to expand their influence and make an impact for the Kingdom in the marketplace.

The Holy Spirit not only helps and aids with our skillset, but the operation of the Gifts of Holy Spirit is also needed in the marketplace:

> Now there are diversities of gifts, but the same Spirit. And **there are differences of administrations**, but the same Lord. And **there are diversities of operations**, but it is the same God which worketh all in all. But **the manifestation of the Spirit is given to every man to profit withal**. For to one is given by the Spirit the word of wisdom; to another the word of knowledge by the same Spirit; to another faith by the same Spirit; to another the gifts of healing by the same Spirit; to another the working of miracles; to another prophecy; to another discerning of spirits; to another divers kinds of tongues; to another the interpretation of tongues: but all these worketh that one and the selfsame Spirit, dividing to every man severally as He will (I Cor. 12:4-10).

It is impossible for every Believer to exercise their gifts at Sunday service. Yet God gave gifts to every man. However, what happens is that God's people will leave the place that they were assigned to and jump from Church to Church looking for the place that will allow them to use their gifts. But here is a truth that you may have never thought of—what if your gift wasn't given to use on Sunday? **Some Believers' gifts only work in the marketplace—because that gift is assigned to the organism and not the institution.** What if the pulpit you are assigned to is at a desk, in a classroom, on a hospital floor, or in a firehouse, but you are saving it all for Sunday? First Corinthians 12:5 says **"there are diversities of administrations."** Joseph was a dream interpreter and a prophet, and not once did he use his gift in the Church. His gift was for government. If we are told to go into the world, then our gifts go too. And it is God's intent that those gifts be used. Mark 16:15-18 says, "And He said unto them, **Go ye into all the world, and preach the Gospel to every creature.** He that believeth and is baptized shall be saved; but he that believeth not shall be damned. **And these signs shall follow them that believe; In My Name shall they cast out devils; they shall speak with new tongues; they shall take up serpents; and if they drink any deadly thing, it shall not hurt them; they shall lay hands on the sick, and they shall recover."** I have a question to ask you—who were all of the things mentioned in the previous verse happening to? The world—the unsaved. All this was happening outside the Church. The unsaved were getting healed. The signs were happening in the life of the unsaved. Miracles were happening to the unsaved. So why are we only operating in our gifts in the Church amongst the saved, when **Jesus gave us the institution for learning and the world to the organism for ministering**? The gifts are for the marketplace as much as they are for the Church: "How God anointed Jesus of Nazareth with the Holy Ghost and with power: **who went about doing good**, and **healing all** that were oppressed of the devil; for God was with Him" (Acts 10:38).

So, why gifts in the marketplace? Because Gifts are an undeniable, irrefutable manifestation of the power and presence of God. And you cannot refute that it's God when the gift does it. The world won't understand the Word, as they don't have the Spirit of God in them. But everyone has a need in their life. If we take our gifts to the marketplace, we give God a place to do His great work there.

Through a gift at work in the marketplace, God gets an opportunity to touch a life that might ordinarily never come to the institution on a Sunday. Are we open to allowing God to do whatever He wants to do however He wants to do it? Or have we allowed tradition and religious thought lock God into a day and lock the Believer out from being able to function at their highest capacity in Him? If Satan sees the marketplace as his mission field, why hasn't the Church?

Jesus to the World

Taking Jesus to the world in business doesn't always mean overtly declaring our faith at the outset but rather demonstrating the values and principles of Christ through our actions. Just as Jesus often allowed His works and fruit to speak for Him, we, too, can reflect Christ in the marketplace in ways that draw people to the Kingdom through our character and the results we produce: **"Therefore, you will fully know them by their fruits" (Mark 7:20 AMPC).** Throughout Jesus's ministry, He often allowed His actions to reveal who He was before He explicitly stated His identity as the Messiah. His miracles, acts of compassion, and wisdom were the primary ways people came to recognize His divine nature. Jesus demonstrated that it was the fruit of His ministry—the healings, miracles, and teaching—that would confirm His identity. People were drawn to Him not by grand declarations, but by the undeniable power and authority of His actions. This principle can also be applied in the business world. We don't always need to announce our faith up front, but rather, we can allow the excellence of our work, the integrity of our leadership, and the compassion with which we treat others to bear witness to the character of Christ in us.

One of the most effective ways to bring Jesus into the world of business is by operating in excellence: **"Then this Daniel was preferred above the presidents and princes, because an excellent spirit was in him; and the king thought to set him over the whole realm" (Dan. 6:3).** When we approach our business endeavors with a mindset of doing everything for the Lord, it elevates our work and sets a standard of excellence that distinguishes us from the rest of the marketplace. Excellence in business reflects Christ because it shows that we value the gifts and opportunities God has given us. When people see the quality of our work, the innovation we bring, or the way we solve problems, they will recognize that something is different about us. This can open doors for conversations about faith without us having to explicitly state it upfront. Just as Jesus's actions spoke louder than words, our business performance can speak to the presence of Christ in us.

Another powerful way to take Jesus into the marketplace is by being people of integrity and honesty. In a business world where cutting corners, unethical practices, and greed are often normalized, operating with honesty and transparency can set Believers apart. Proverbs 11:3 NIV says, **"The integrity of the upright guides them, but the unfaithful are destroyed by their duplicity."** Believers should be dependable and people who keep their word. You should be known as a truth-teller, and someone who always stays on the side of right. Sometimes this may come with scrutiny; however, you are known as someone who will always do what's right and say what's right: **"In all things shewing thyself a pattern of good works: in doctrine shewing uncorruptness, gravity, sincerity, sound speech, that cannot be condemned; that he that is of the contrary part may be ashamed, having no evil thing to say of you" (Tit. 2:7-8).** Jesus modeled this kind of integrity throughout His ministry. He was consistent in His words and actions, and people trusted Him because they saw that He was truthful and upright. In business, integrity means keeping your word, treating people fairly, and doing the right thing even when no one is watching. When we lead with integrity, it reflects the heart of Christ, and others will take notice.

Jesus also demonstrated the importance of service and compassion in His approach to people. He was always concerned with meeting the needs of others, whether healing the sick, feeding the hungry, or comforting the brokenhearted. This same heart for service can be carried into the marketplace. Matthew 20:28 says, **"Just as the Son of Man did not come to be served, but to serve, and to give His**

life as a ransom for many." In business, service can take the form of going above and beyond for clients, creating products that genuinely help people, or fostering a workplace culture that prioritizes the well-being of employees. When we approach business with a servant's heart, we reflect the love of Christ to those around us. People will be drawn to do business with us not just because of what we offer but because of how we operate, with kindness, empathy, and a genuine desire to serve.

The Bible calls us to bear fruit that reflects the character of God, and this applies in business as much as in any other area of life. Galatians 5:22-23 lists the fruit of the Spirit: **"But the fruit of the Spirit is love, joy, peace, forbearance, kindness, goodness, faithfulness, gentleness and self-control."** When we display these characteristics in our interactions with employees, clients, and business partners, we show the world who Christ is through our actions. For example, exercising patience and kindness in difficult negotiations or showing gentleness and self-control in high-pressure situations speaks volumes about our character and who we serve. People will notice that we operate differently from the cutthroat, profit-driven mentality of the world. When we allow the fruit of the Spirit to shape how we conduct business, it creates a powerful testimony to the presence of Christ in our lives.

> When we lead with integrity, it reflects the heart of Christ, and others will take notice.

Jesus taught that His followers are to be the light of the world, and that light should shine brightly in the business realm. Matthew 5:16 says, **"In the same way, let your light shine before others, that they may see your good deeds and glorify your Father in heaven."** Our "good deeds" in business, whether they are acts of service, leadership, or innovation, are opportunities to reflect God's glory. By focusing on the quality of our work, how we treat others, and how we conduct ourselves, we allow the light of Christ to shine through us. This doesn't always require us to preach openly or overtly identify as Christians at the start. Like Jesus, we can let our fruit speak for us, and in time, those we encounter in business will recognize that we carry something different—something divine.

Taking Jesus to the world in business means reflecting His character and principles in all that we do. Just as Jesus performed great works and allowed those works to testify to His identity, we, too, can allow the fruit of our work, integrity, service, and compassion to reveal Christ to those around us. By leading with excellence, honesty, and a heart to serve, we become ambassadors for Christ in the marketplace, bringing the presence and power of the Kingdom into the business world. Our actions and the fruit of our labor will draw others to ask, "What is different about you?"—allowing Christ to be shared.

Chapter 9

Biblical Principles in the Marketplace

Each of these principles provides a biblical foundation for conducting business with excellence and integrity. When you apply these principles in your business, you honor God and position yourself for long-term success.

1. Timeliness

- **Principle:** Be diligent in your work and honor deadlines, knowing that timely action brings reward.
- **Scripture:** "Take a lesson from the ants, you lazybones. Learn from their ways and become wise! Though they have no prince or governor or ruler to make them work, they labor hard all summer, gathering food for the winter" (Prov. 6:6-8 NLT).
- **Application:** Timeliness in business, like the ants in Proverbs, is a reflection of discipline and foresight. Meeting deadlines and being proactive ensures that opportunities are seized and resources are used effectively.

2. Confidence

- **Principle:** Approach business endeavors with confidence, knowing that God empowers you for success.

- **Scripture:** "I can do all things through Christ who gives me strength" (Phil. 4:13 NLT).
- **Application:** As a Christian in business, your confidence should stem from your reliance on God's strength and not just your own abilities. God equips you for every challenge and opportunity, allowing you to walk boldly in the marketplace.

3. The Use of Godly Wisdom

- **Principle:** Always seek God's wisdom in business decisions, trusting His guidance for success and protection from errors.
- **Scripture:** "If you need wisdom, ask our generous God, and he will give it to you. He will not rebuke you for asking" (James 1:5 NLT).
- **Application:** Godly wisdom is essential for navigating the complexities of business. Seeking God's guidance will help you make sound decisions, avoid pitfalls, and capitalize on opportunities in alignment with His will.

4. Stewardship

- **Principle:** Be faithful in managing the resources, time, and people God has entrusted to you.
- **Scripture:** "And if you are untrustworthy about worldly wealth, who will trust you with the true riches of heaven?" (Luke 16:11 NLT).
- **Application:** Stewardship in business involves responsible management of finances, employees, and opportunities. God blesses those who are diligent and trustworthy with what He has given, preparing them for greater responsibilities.

5. Going the Extra Mile

- **Principle:** Serve others in business by going beyond the bare minimum, demonstrating excellence and generosity.
- **Scripture:** "If a soldier demands that you carry his gear for a mile, carry it two miles" (Matt. 5:41 NLT).

- **Application:** Going the extra mile is a principle of servant leadership. It reflects a heart of service, integrity, and excellence, making you stand out in the marketplace and building long-lasting relationships with clients, employees, and partners.

6. Management

- **Principle:** Lead and manage people with fairness, wisdom, and diligence, knowing that effective leadership honors God and promotes growth.

- **Scripture:** "A wise ruler knows how to bring order; an incompetent leader ruins everything" (Prov. 29:4 NLT).

- **Application:** Effective management in business requires godly wisdom, clear communication, and fair treatment of all employees. Proper leadership not only brings order and efficiency but also helps cultivate a healthy work environment where people can thrive.

7. Integrity

- **Principle:** Operate your business with honesty and integrity, always doing what is right, even when no one is watching.
- **Verse:** "The godly walk with integrity; blessed are their children who follow them" (Prov. 20:7 NLT).
- **Application:** Operate your business with moral uprightness and honesty, doing what is right even when no one is watching. Make decisions that align with your values and ensure that your business practices reflect ethical standards.

8. Diligence

- **Principle:** Hard work, perseverance, and careful planning lead to success.
- **Verse:** "Good planning and hard work lead to prosperity, but hasty shortcuts lead to poverty" (Prov. 21:5 NLT).

- **Application:** Work hard, be consistent, and persevere in your efforts. Diligence helps you remain focused on your goals, ensuring that tasks are completed with care and efficiency, which leads to long-term success.

9. Generosity

- **Principle:** Be generous in business dealings, sharing the blessings God has given you with others.
- **Verse:** "Give, and you will receive. Your gift will return to you in full, pressed down, shaken together to make room for more, running over, and poured into your lap. The amount you give will determine the amount you get back" (Luke 6:38 NLT).
- **Application:** Share your resources, time, money, and expertise, freely with others. This can take the form of fair wages for employees, donations to charitable causes, or offering assistance to those in need.

10. Wisdom

- **Principle:** Seek God's wisdom in all business decisions, knowing that His wisdom leads to success.
- **Verse:** "If you need wisdom, ask our generous God, and he will give it to you. He will not rebuke you for asking" (James 1:5 NLT).
- **Application:** Seek divine wisdom in your business decisions, using both practical knowledge and spiritual discernment. Wisdom ensures that your choices are aligned with God's will and lead to success.

11. Faithfulness

- **Principle:** Be faithful in the small things, and God will entrust you with greater responsibility.
- **Verse:** "If you are faithful in little things, you will be faithful in large ones. But if you are dishonest in little things, you won't be honest with greater responsibilities" (Luke 16:10 NLT).

- **Application:** Be reliable, consistent, and loyal in your commitments. Faithfulness fosters trust among employees, clients, and partners, and it demonstrates that you can be depended upon in all circumstances.

12. Honesty

- **Principle:** Conduct all business with truth and transparency.
- **Verse:** "The Lord detests the use of dishonest scales, but he delights in accurate weights" (Prov. 11:1 NLT).
- **Application:** Be transparent and truthful in all business dealings. Honesty builds a foundation of trust with clients, employees, and stakeholders, ensuring that your business stands out for its integrity.

13. Humility

- **Principle:** Lead with humility, understanding that pride leads to downfall but humility brings honor.
- **Verse:** "Pride leads to disgrace, but with humility comes wisdom" (Prov. 11:2 NLT).
- **Application:** Lead with a spirit of humility, putting others before yourself and recognizing that success comes from God's grace, not personal ability. Humility in leadership fosters collaboration and a healthy workplace culture.

14. Planning

- **Principle:** Make wise and strategic plans, but always commit your plans to the Lord for His blessing.
- **Verse:** "Commit your actions to the Lord, and your plans will succeed" (Prov. 16:3 NLT).
- **Application:** Carefully plan and prepare for the future, understanding that wise planning reduces risk and increases the likelihood of success. But also, commit your plans to God for His direction.

15. Justice and Fairness

- **Principle:** Treat employees, clients, and business partners with fairness and justice.
- **Verse:** "The Lord demands accurate scales and balances; he sets the standards for fairness" (Prov. 16:11 NLT).
- **Application:** Treat all people, employees, clients, and partners, fairly and justly. Upholding fairness ensures equality in how decisions are made and prevents exploitation or favoritism.

16. Patience

- **Principle:** Success in business often takes time and requires patience.
- **Verse:** "Better to be patient than powerful; better to have self-control than to conquer a city" (Prov. 16:32 NLT).
- **Application:** Exercise patience in both business growth and decision-making. Success often takes time, and rushing through decisions or expecting quick results can lead to poor outcomes.

17. Accountability

- **Principle:** Be accountable for your actions, ensuring your business dealings align with God's standards.
- **Verse:** "People who conceal their sins will not prosper, but if they confess and turn from them, they will receive mercy" (Prov. 28:13 NLT).
- **Application:** Hold yourself and your team accountable for actions and outcomes. Accountability fosters responsibility and ensures that everyone is working toward the same goals with transparency and integrity.

18. Excellence

- **Principle:** Strive for excellence in all that you do, giving your best effort in everything.

- **Verse:** "Work willingly at whatever you do, as though you were working for the Lord rather than for people" (Col. 3:23 NLT)
- **Application:** Strive for excellence in every aspect of your business, from product quality to customer service. Excellence honors God and reflects His nature of perfection.

19. Servant Leadership

- **Principle:** Lead by serving others, following Jesus's example of servant leadership.
- **Verse:** "But among you it will be different. Whoever wants to be a leader among you must be your servant" (Matt. 20:26 NLT)
- **Application:** Lead by serving others—your employees, customers, and community. Servant leadership prioritizes the well-being and development of others over personal gain, fostering loyalty and trust.

20. Trust in God's Provision

- **Principle:** Trust God for provision in your business, knowing that He will supply all your needs.
- **Verse:** "And this same God who takes care of me will supply all your needs from his glorious riches, which have been given to us in Christ Jesus" (Phil. 4:19 NLT).
- **Application:** In business, trust that God will supply all your needs—finances, resources, or opportunities. Rather than striving out of fear, operate with confidence, knowing that God is your provider and sustainer.

21. Forgiveness

- **Principle:** Be quick to forgive offenses and resolve conflicts in a way that honors God.

- **Verse:** Instead, be kind to each other, tenderhearted, forgiving one another, just as God through Christ has forgiven you" (Eph. 4:32 NLT).
- **Application:** Quickly forgive those who wrong you in the marketplace—whether it's a business partner, employee, or client. Holding grudges and harboring bitterness can poison relationships and stall progress. Forgiveness restores peace and moves business relationships forward.

22. Unity and Teamwork

- **Principle:** Promote unity and collaboration within your team, understanding the power of working together.
- **Verse:** "Make every effort to keep yourselves united in the Spirit, binding yourselves together with peace" (Eph. 4:3 NLT).
- **Application:** Promote unity and collaboration within your team, understanding that success comes through working together. A united team is more innovative, productive, and able to face challenges effectively.

23. Contentment

- **Principle:** Be content with what you have while working diligently to grow.
- **Verse:** "Yet true godliness with contentment is itself great wealth" (1 Tim. 6:6 NLT).
- **Application:** Be content with what God has provided while still working diligently toward growth. Contentment keeps you grounded and prevents unhealthy striving for more at the cost of peace and integrity.

24. Perseverance

- **Principle:** Persevere through challenges, trusting that God will provide strength to overcome obstacles.

- **Verse:** "So let's not get tired of doing what is good. At just the right time we will reap a harvest of blessing if we don't give up" (Gal. 6:9 NLT)
- **Application:** Persevere through business challenges, trusting that success often comes through persistence and faithfulness. Setbacks and failures are part of the journey, but continuing in faith leads to eventual breakthrough.

25. Rest and Renewal

- **Principle:** Embrace times of rest and renewal, knowing that God values both work and rest.
- **Verse:** "Then Jesus said, 'Come to me, all of you who are weary and carry heavy burdens, and I will give you rest'" (Matt. 11:28 NLT)
- **Application:** Recognize the importance of rest and renewal for sustained success. Both physical rest and spiritual renewal are essential for long-term productivity and creativity in business. Resting in God's presence refreshes your mind and spirit, allowing you to lead from a place of peace.

26. Faith

- **Principle:** Trust God completely in your business endeavors, believing that He will provide guidance, resources, and favor to succeed in the marketplace. Faith in God allows you to move forward with confidence, even when the outcome is uncertain.
- **Verse:** "Trust in the Lord with all your heart; do not depend on your own understanding. Seek his will in all you do, and he will show you which path to take" (Prov. 3:5-6 NLT).
- **Application:** In business, faith empowers you to take risks, pursue new opportunities, and make decisions that align with God's direction, even when the path ahead isn't clear. Trusting in God's provision and wisdom gives you the confidence to act boldly while knowing that He is ultimately in control of the outcomes. Faith ensures that your business decisions are

grounded in a dependence on God's guidance rather than your own abilities or market conditions.

27. Honoring Commitment

- **Principle:** Keep your word and fulfill your promises in all business dealings. Honoring commitments builds trust, establishes a strong reputation, and reflects integrity in the marketplace.
- **Verse**: "Just say a simple, 'Yes, I will,' or 'No, I won't.' Anything beyond this is from the evil one" (Matt. 5:37 NLT).
- **Application:** In business, honoring commitments means being reliable and following through on promises to clients, partners, and employees. It involves delivering on contracts, meeting deadlines, and maintaining ethical practices. When you keep your word, you build trust with those around you, establish credibility, and demonstrate integrity, which leads to long-term success and stronger relationships in the marketplace.

Chapter 10

Gifts of the Spirit in the Marketplace

The Gifts of the Spirit can be powerfully applied in the marketplace. They guide leaders in making God-honoring decisions, fostering healthy relationships, and building businesses that reflect Kingdom values. When you apply these gifts and principles, your business will not only thrive but also shine as a testimony of God's wisdom and grace in the world.

Wisdom (Word of Wisdom)

- **Application:** In business strategy and decision-making, the gift of wisdom helps you see beyond the present circumstances, giving insight for long-term planning and innovative solutions. This divine wisdom can guide critical business decisions, partnerships, and investments.
- **Example:** Leaders can apply wisdom when navigating complex negotiations, seeking God's guidance to create win-win scenarios.

Knowledge (Word of Knowledge)

- **Application:** The gift of knowledge allows you to understand facts and situations supernaturally. In the marketplace, it can reveal important insights into a problem, an opportunity, or even a client's needs that wouldn't be known otherwise.

- **Example:** A business leader might receive a prompting about a specific market trend or client need that provides a competitive edge or key solution.

Faith

- **Application:** The gift of faith empowers leaders to trust God in the face of overwhelming challenges, such as launching new ventures, entering new markets, or overcoming financial crises. It emboldens believers to take risks based on God's promises.
- **Example:** Entrepreneurs can utilize the gift of faith when starting new businesses or expanding into unknown territories, trusting God for provision and guidance.

Healing

- **Application:** While often seen in physical healing, this gift can also be applied in a workplace environment to foster emotional or relational healing. It helps resolve conflict, restores broken relationships among employees or partners, and brings peace.
- **Example:** A manager might use the gift of healing to bring reconciliation to a conflict-ridden team, helping restore trust and collaboration.

Miracles

- **Application:** Miracles in business might manifest as unexpected breakthroughs, sudden financial provision, or overcoming impossible odds. This gift empowers leaders to believe in and witness the supernatural intervention of God in seemingly hopeless situations.
- **Example:** A business on the brink of collapse might experience miraculous recovery through unforeseen opportunities or resources that come through divine intervention.

Prophecy

- **Application:** The gift of prophecy in business can bring clarity and direction. Prophetic insight helps leaders know which opportunities to pursue, what markets to enter, and how to align business goals with God's purposes.

- **Example:** A leader might receive prophetic insight about future market shifts, guiding them to prepare for upcoming trends or avoid potential risks.

Discerning of Spirits

- **Application:** The ability to discern the spiritual dynamics at play helps leaders recognize deceptive practices, unethical business deals, or partnerships that may seem promising but are harmful.
- **Example:** A business owner might discern hidden agendas or dishonesty in a potential partnership and avoid it, thereby protecting the business from harm.

Speaking in Tongues

- **Application:** While speaking in tongues is often a private form of prayer, it can be used by leaders in the marketplace to pray for divine strategies, guidance, and direction when facing difficult situations or decisions.
- **Example:** In moments of uncertainty, a leader may pray in tongues for divine insight before making a crucial business decision.

Interpretation of Tongues

- **Application:** This gift is used in partnership with speaking in tongues to understand the direction or insight God is revealing. It can provide specific answers or strategies for business situations when the normal course of understanding is limited.

- **Example:** After praying in tongues, a leader receives clear interpretation, offering divine strategies for business challenges.

Conclusion

Luke 19:13 states, "So he called ten of his servants and gave them ten minas. 'Put this money to work,' he said, 'until I come back.'" This directive from Jesus is not just a spiritual metaphor but a clear mandate for engagement in the real world, including the business world. It's a call to action for Believers to be bold, strategic, and intentional in using their gifts and resources to influence the marketplace for God's glory. For the modern Christian business leader, the message is clear: it's time to fully embrace the marketplace as a mission field and an opportunity to advance God's Kingdom.

For too long, many in the Church have seen the business world as disconnected from spiritual impact. But the marketplace is where innovation, leadership, and influence converge to shape culture and society. Businesses have the power to drive change, create wealth, and set ethical standards that reflect Kingdom values. God's call to "occupy till I come" (Luke 19:13) means that we are to be active participants in the world of commerce, entrepreneurship, and leadership, not just for personal gain but to make a lasting impact for God.

By stepping into the marketplace with purpose, Christian business leaders can model integrity, lead with vision, and bring innovative solutions to complex problems, all while advancing the values of God's Kingdom. This is about more than making money; it's about using business as a platform to bring about positive change, build communities, and influence industries.

The marketplace offers unparalleled opportunities for Believers to create a lasting legacy, not just through products and services, but through the way they lead and operate. Now is the time to be bold, to invest your talents, and to use your business as a vehicle for greater Kingdom impact. God has given you the skills, resources, and opportunities to make a difference. Not only that, but we have an order to, "Go ye in to all the world," (Mark 16:15) and that this Gospel of the Kingdom of God is to be preached to all the world as a witness.

There are people who have yet to stop foot inside of the institution, so God uses the other arm of the Church, the organism, to reach them. These two arms are not independent of each other but codependent for the victory of sharing with the lost. In addition, the call to "occupy" is a call to take ownership of your role in the marketplace and to lead with excellence, demonstrating the power and purpose of a Kingdom-minded business. The time is now for Christian business leaders to embrace the marketplace fully, leading with boldness, vision, and integrity to advance God's Kingdom and reclaim areas of influence for His glory.

Acknowledgements

I am never alone in anything that I do. It takes a team, and I have one of the best.

To MiShondia, my amazing wife and partner in ministry. It's a Kingdom journey that I am honored to share with you.

To Joe, Kirah, and Kennedy. I am eternally grateful to have my children serving we me in ministry. You are a tremendous blessing. To see your spiritual growth is truly inspiriting. Thanks for all you help and support.

To Olivia, Rosalyn and John. You are the best. It is your unwavering and consistent contribution that makes us who we are as a Church. You are my A-team! Thank you for your support, love, patience and push.

To the amazing members of Right Way Christian Center. God has shown Himself faithful and brought us a long way. I am even the more excited to see where God is taking us.

To my Lord and Savior. Thank You for entrusting me to the gift to scribe, and lead Your people as a pastor. I am fully surrendered and eternally grateful for the assignment and I fully commit to growing Your people in Christ the right way.

Notes

1. Robert F. Smith, https://robertfsmith.org/news/, about-robert-f-smith/
2. Forbes - Purpose-Driven Business Models Propel Faith-Based Efforts, Rod Berger, June 23,2023, https://www.forbes.com/sites/rodberger/2023/01/23/purpose-driven-business-models-propel-faith-based-efforts/ Timothy Cahill, Yale Divinity School Forbes.
3. https://www.weforum.org/stories/2022/11/4-ways-purpose-into-profitability/

Don't Miss These Additional Ministry Tools from Vincent Robinson!

LEADer explains the character and integrity that is needed to lead and not just the skill and system.

ISBN: 978-1-7360064-5-0

Kingdom Philanthropy is for Christian businesspeople on financing God's Kingdom business and a wake-up to those gifted to the Church as Kingdom philanthropists.

ISBN: 978-1-7360064-7-4

vincent robinson ministries

Learn more at:
vrministries.org

ɿs, we have an earthly
ɿment that we should fulfill, ɛ
ɜs wealth to accomplish it.

KINGDOM WEALTH
A Primer of Wealth and
rosperity For the Believer

ɿey does not have to be a mɛ
hard thing in life if we woulc
elop the discipline of stewarc
selves properly.

ree Gift!!

Made in the USA
Monee, IL
04 November 2026

67374667R00098